AFRICAN SEASONS

Wildlife at the Waterhole

An elephant mourns a dead relative.

AFRICAN SEASONS

Wildlife at the Waterhole

CRAIG BONE
Written by Alistair Chambers

PB

PARKGATE
BOOKS

This book is dedicated to Adrian
Hamilton; without his help and support
this project would never have got
off the ground.

ACKNOWLEDGEMENTS
Thanks to the people who helped (in all sorts of
ways) to make this book possible: Mr Bertran
Owen Smith (S.R.C.S.), Anne-Marie Bone, Stan
Fourie, Kelvin Hein, Bob Graves, Ian Bunnett,
Meg Coates Palgrave and Liz Radford.

First published in 1993

This edition published in 1997 by
Parkgate Books Ltd
London House, Great Eastern Wharf
Parkgate Road, London SW11 4NQ
Great Britain

2 4 6 8 9 7 5 3 1

Editors Liz Radford and Helen Varley
Designer Tom Deas
Art Director Dave Allen
Editorial Director Pippa Rubinstein

**The Catalogue record for this book is available
from the British Library**

ISBN 1 85585 340 X

Printed in Italy

CONTENTS

INTRODUCTION

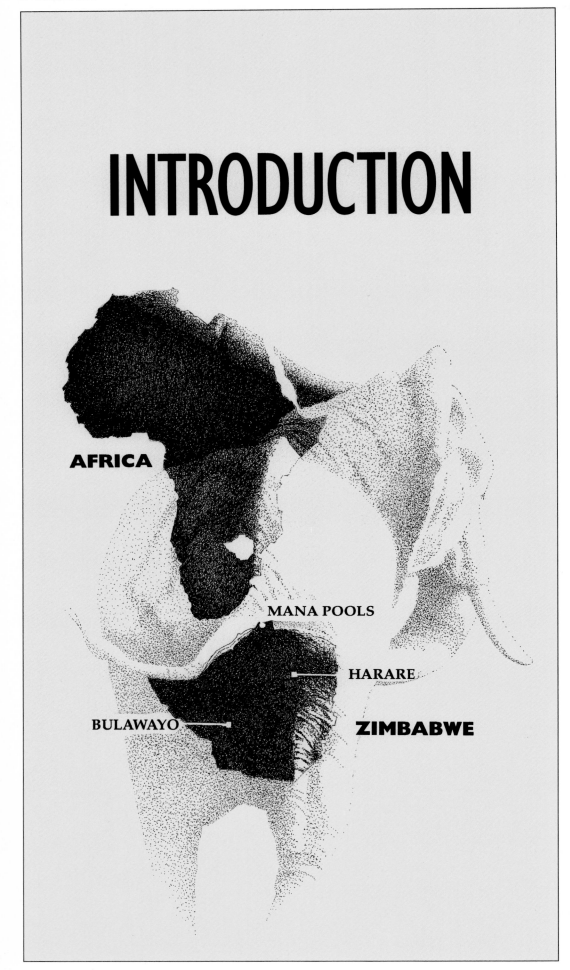

AFRICA

MANA POOLS

HARARE

BULAWAYO

ZIMBABWE

THE ORIGINS OF MANA POOLS

THE ZAMBEZI

Millions of years ago the earth's crust tore apart in a cataclysmic eruption, forming a great rift 4,000 miles (6,400 kilometres) long. The healing of this rift left great scars across the earth's surface – the Red Sea, and the Great Rift Valley that runs southward through Kenya in East Africa to Mozambique. The rift splintered westwards, diverting the Zambezi River from its course – probably through Botswana – and redirecting it along the rift valley. Today, the Zambezi forms the boundary between Zambia to the north and Zimbabwe to the south, before flowing eastward through Mozambique to the Indian Ocean.

Just inside Zimbabwe, the river plunges 350 feet (108 metres) to form the spectacular Victoria Falls. Below the Falls, the river rushes through stunning gorges in frenzied fury – making this stretch of white water Africa's most exciting rafting and kayaking run. At the gorge's end the river flows into the tranquil Lake Kariba. This huge reservoir covers an area of some 2,000 square miles (5,000 square kilometres), so that on completion it became the largest man-made lake in the world.

The Zambezi is a lifeline for southern Africa. It provides power: the huge turbines on the Kariba dam wall supply Zimbabwe and Zambia with most of their hydro-electric power. Soon the river waters will be pumped to drought-stricken areas. Fisheries have been established in Kariba's peaceful waters, and the lake is a haven for wildlife.

The river flows on through the Kariba Gorge, which ends abruptly, opening into the Zambezi valley, which ranges between eighteen and thirty miles (thirty to fifty kilometres) in width on the Zimbabwe side. Downstream there is an area where the river used to flood its banks during heavy rains, forming a large, fertile floodplain. A small section of this floodplain was so rich in flora and fauna that it was declared a National Park, and given the name Mana Pools.

MANA POOLS

Mana Pools covers some 850 square miles (2,200 square kilometres) and was designated a National Park in 1963. At around the same time, Zambia also gave the floodplain on the northern bank National Park status. Today, the Zambezi is the only one of Africa's four large rivers with its natural flora and fauna still intact. Fortunately the powers-that-be have recognized the need to preserve areas like these. It is right that future generations should be able to admire the staggering beauty of this region. And this is the main reason why, in 1985, UNESCO declared Mana Pools a World Heritage site.

After many years of living in Mana Pools, observing, photographing and painting the many different plants and living creatures, and their fascinating interaction, we felt it was time to share our experiences.

The Mana Pools area of the Zambezi valley consists of four permanently filled pools, and a number of smaller seasonal pans, or waterholes, on their fringes.

One day, as Craig Bone sat in his hide beside one of these waterholes, photographing the animals and birds that came to drink there, the tranquillity was shattered by the noise of an approaching vehicle.

The wildlife bombshelled. Doves whistled by overhead. Impala triple-jumped away. Baboons leaped from trees like falling trapeze artists. The engine stopped. The alien noise changed – to the voices of the intruders: `Nothing here. Maybe we should try Mucheni again'.

After the vibrations of the motor had faded away, the bush sounds gradually started up once more. The doves signalled the all-clear in song, and flew to the water's edge. The squirrel came out of hiding. The kingfisher stayed on the perch he had not moved from at the height of the intrusion. A small crocodile continued to camouflage himself as a log. Ideas began ticking over in the artist's head.

Through this book we hope to show people the many things that they often fail to see: how the various interactions of the wild work and, most importantly, the pyramid of life.

STRIKING A BALANCE

Water is the vital element around which all life revolves. The Sapi Waterhole – where Craig was hiding while the intruders came and went – provides the setting for this book. After the rains, the waterhole overflows with life-giving water; in the dry months it shrinks to a mosaic pattern of cracked mud. The life of the waterhole changes accordingly. For some species, survival becomes more difficult; for others the dangers are reduced.

Nature has developed a perfect biological balance in the natural world. From the elephant to

the termite, each form of life is dependent on another. Looking at the bush, all dry grass, sandy soil and fallen trees, it is difficult to imagine that anything could survive there. Yet this apparently hostile environment supports thousands of life forms. Each has its unique strategy for survival.

The following pages illustrate some of the more interesting methods nature utilizes in the daily battle for existence. ∎

Newly born sable are a tawny colour, and blend in with the bush. Their colour and their scruffy coat (which breaks up their outline), enable them to avoid detection when separated from their mother.

THE HABITATS

Halfway along its course to the Indian Ocean the Zambezi River passes through the depression known as the Zambezi valley. In this valley is one of Africa's last wildlife strongholds, Mana Pools. The exact location of Mana Pools is shown on the map on page 6, and its formation and designation as a National Park and a UNESCO World Heritage Site, has already been described.

The name Mana Pools refers to the many pools, both permanent and seasonal, that are to be found in this floodplain area. Mana Pools may be divided into three main habitat types for wildlife: the jesse bush; the mopane woodland; and the floodplain. On the next few pages we look at each of these in turn. ■

The flap-neck chameleon is greatly feared by many tribes, and is the subject of much folklore.

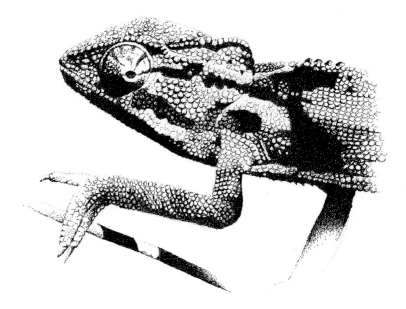

THE JESSE BUSH

The name 'jesse' is a collective term used to describe the various shrubs, large bushes, scrambling bushes, and climbers – any of which may be armed with wicked thorns – that grow closely together to form large areas of this often impenetrable scrub. This habitat type is always found on sandy soils and many nutritious plants are found within it. One plant-type, Baphia (for example, *Baphia massaiensis*), contains more crude protein than alfalfa (lucerne), the highly nutritious fodder crop.

Due to its density, the jesse needs an extensive road network that functions like the network of routes connecting the different areas of a large city. This network is created largely by elephants, who are also partly responsible for laying the side-streets; but the rhinos and buffalo help. The road network gives the animals access everywhere, while the thicket forms an ideal retreat, and a refuge during daylight hours.

Some of these paths are elephant trails, which can go in a straight line for many miles, usually from one waterhole to the next. You have to marvel at the sense of direction of these amazing bush engineers. In fact, when walking from the valley floor up into the escarpment, there is never any better way to get to the top than by following an elephant trail. These animals always follow an even gradient, not too steep, and frequently use spurs and outcrops on their way to the top. Some Zimbabwean engineers siting a road down an escarpment are said to have followed an elephant trail almost exactly.

The jesse supplies a number of advantages for the animals that live in it. The buffalo lie up in it to rest, quietly chewing their cud, the shade providing them with welcome relief during the heat of the day. It is practically impossible to get close to these animals – even if you knew where they were in the first place. Hunters who are fortunate enough to get near buffalo in jesse find it difficult to get a clear shot, and then the bullets are easily deflected by the maze of twigs around. Normally, the only time you know you are near to animals in the jesse is when you hear them crashing away ahead of you. Adrenalin flows as a disturbed herd suddenly takes off. Not knowing in what direction they are stampeding is a bit unsettling. An animal will only become visible a few yards away – and if an angry cow manages to find you, you can kiss your bottom goodbye! ■

This lioness has dragged her meat into the cover of the jesse. Lions can eat 75 lb (35 kg) of meat if hungry. The liver of the carcass provides the lion with Vitamin A, which – like other cats, it cannot produce itself.

MOPANE WOODLAND

After catching a small fish, the pied kingfisher beats its prey to death on a perch before swallowing.

The soils on which the mopane trees grow are notoriously poor. In places they are very heavily clay-based, making them a hell for even four-wheel drive vehicles to traverse during the hot wet season. Relatively few species and varieties of plants can grow on these soils, so the mopane trees dominate; hence the name of this type of woodland.

Mopane trees grow only in Africa, and are normally to be found in hot, low-lying areas. The wood is extremely hard, and much prized by locals as firewood. The leaves are shaped like butterfly wings, and between the wings is a third vestigial leaf. The leaves are aromatic (we can only describe the smell as like that of a mixture of turpentine and camphor!) and are always refreshing to smell.

If there are no encroaching shrubs, this woodland can be very open, because the trees have fairly sparse canopies, starting high up on the trunk. The lack of tree diversity means that mopane woodland houses fewer species of birds, mammals, and insects than either the jesse or the floodplain. It does, however, provide valuable browsing for animals, particularly at the end of the dry season, when the mopanes are among the first trees in flush. The dry leaves of the mopane contain sufficient crude protein to make them edible at these times. The trees are highly valued by elephants, who spend much time feeding on them, mostly at night. They feed at this time because they do not feel too secure in this open woodland during the day, when they are much more visible.

Mopane is very pretty woodland, and it is highly important in the region because of the numbers of waterholes, many of them perennial, that may be found in it. The clay base makes their water retention good. At these waterholes beautiful trees, such as the big jackalberry, tamarinds and nyalaberries, are usually to be found. These trees provide welcome shade in the baking heat at noon, and their fruits ripen during the lean time of the year.

The mopane tree has a tenant in the form of a caterpillar. This caterpillar is the product of the eggs laid by the mopane moth (*Gonimbrasia belina*), which are laid during spring-time (November). These caterpillars grow to about three inches (seven centimetres), and are a great delicacy for the indigenous people. After having been plucked from the trees, they are dried, and stored to be eaten later. ∎

Mopane woodland. Elephants enjoy feeding on mopane trees, and can reach up to eighteen feet (five and a half metres). They tend to feed at night, as they feel vulnerable during the day in the open woodland.

THE FLOODPLAIN

The pangolin's stomach contains grit to aid in grinding up food for digestion. It rolls into a tight ball for protection.

This is the area people usually associate with Mana Pools. Within the National Park, it consists of less than thirty square miles (eighty square kilometres). Before Kariba Dam was built (just upstream from Mana Pools), this area flooded during heavy rains. This flooding fertilized the land, and so there was great concern that the damming of the river would deny these lower regions their much-needed seed distribution and 'fertilizer'.

Long ago the Zambezi ran a different course in Mana, and the pools now remaining betray the course of the old river route. Similar to a mining operation, the Zambezi River dug away at the northern banks, throwing the soil (silt) behind it. Trapped by this silt, stretches of the old river remained behind. These orphaned channels of water soon became pools, or oxbow lakes. There are four main pools, the largest of which is called Long Pool, and this is some two miles (three kilometres) long. These pools are believed to have given the region its name, because 'Mana' is probably a derivative of the Shona word 'ina', meaning four. Shona is the most widely spoken language in Zimbabwe. The largest 'tribe' in Zimbabwe is the Mashonas, of Mashonaland province, and they speak this language.

With each season of heavy rain the Zambezi used to flood its banks here, the flood waters creeping back some two miles (three kilometres) to the remnants of the river's old bank. This area still provides sanctuary for the many animals that migrate here as the bush dries out inland. It is very fertile and supplies grazing and browsing possibilities when there is little elsewhere.

The fertile alluvial soils also support the beautiful *Faidherbia albida* trees (formerly known as *Acacia albida*), which dominate the area, forming in places an almost unbroken canopy. These trees are the only ones out here (that we know of) that drop their leaves in summer, and in winter, when most of the other trees have dropped theirs, burst into leaf to give plentiful shade. At the same time they produce pods resembling an apple ring, hence the common name for the tree, apple-ring acacia. These curly seedpods provide much-needed protein in the lean winter period, and are the favoured food of the elephant.

The elephants are seen in greater numbers just before the rains, moving quietly from tree to tree. Along with the elephants come the impala, who are responsible for denuding the area of grass during this period. In fact, at this time of year, impala seem to be everywhere. When first arriving in Mana a visitor will say, 'Oh look, there are impalas – how exciting!' Towards the end of his stay the same visitor might be asked if he has seen anything on the game drive: 'No, not really', would probably be the reply. This does 'God's little goats' (as the Africans call them) an injustice, but you find even the most hardened city dwellers soon get bored seeing so many of them. ■

Termites, which build mounds like these, are part of the life cycle of the wild. They keep the soil fertile by continually stirring it up; and they also aerate the soil to let water penetrate easily through numerous holes,

thus preventing run-off and resulting soil erosion. Faidherbia albida trees are very common on the floodplain. One tree can produce over 660 lb (300 kg) of pods, and these pods are dropped between August and

October. Unfortunately, the albida trees are an endangered species because regrowth from seed shedding is minimal, and the elephants feed on them.

The time is midday, the time of year June. Sable antelope (a rare sight at Mana Pools) are drinking at a pan - a waterhole inland from the Zambezi River. In the background a herd of young bull elephants is unhurriedly making its way down to the banks of the Zambezi. In the late afternoon the elephants might wade over to feed on islands in the river.

Leopard cubs practise their stalking skills.

THE SEASONS

Zimbabwe is blessed with a beautiful climate because of its altitude, which results in it enjoying temperatures similar to those of temperate latitudes.

For five months of the year we have a rainy season, the remaining months are dry. This yearly cycle can be better divided into four seasonal changes. Firstly, there is a cool dry season, from May to mid-August; next is a hot dry season – mid-August to October; this is followed by a rainy season, from November to March; with the final, cool, post-rainy season occurring from April to May.

The average rainy season lasts from late October/early November until March/April. High- and low-pressure systems moving eastward past the South African coast control the weather fluctuations. The days become warmer and more moist when the pressure falls, and the winds develop a northern influence. If this pressure rise is quick then the winds become south-easterly, and cooler, more moist air enters the southernmost regions of the country. The inter-tropical convergence zone (ITCZ – see page 64) comes into effect after October and is an important influence on weather patterns. From December to March this ITCZ, combined with the powerful tropical cyclones in the Mozambique Channel interrelate with the southern pressure changes. Whenever the ITCZ is formed over Zimbabwe there are thunderstorms, and rain distribution. This rain is reduced if there is a cyclone in the Mozambique Channel, because dry south-east upper winds spread over the country instead. Should this same cyclone move inland the rain will increase. If the ITCZ moves northwards we experience a short bout of rain, but this soon peters out. The ITCZ can move further northwards if cold air occurs around March, and this can drastically shorten the rainy season.

In May the country experiences a drop in temperature, with cold nights and sunny, warm days. Towards the end of August temperatures start to rise, along with higher winds. These winds get stronger in September and October, with a corresponding rise in temperature and humidity. The violent thunderstorms start in the latter part of this period and this is a time of great concern for the country, as the antiquated power system often cannot cope with direct lightning strikes, which cause frequent power cuts and a number of fatalities; Zimbabwe has been recorded as suffering the most deaths ever to occur from a single lightning strike (21 people in Mutare in 1975). These thunderstorms peak in November, with their accompanying deluges of rain. The thunderstorms gradually decline and give way to gentler, rainy spells. By April this rain is mixed with periods of hot spells. This period, from November to April, is one of mild temperatures with much promise of rains. The post-April period is a refreshing time, with good visibility, mild temperatures and clear evening skies.

If Zimbabwe experiences less than seventy per cent of normal rainfall then this is regarded as a drought, and occurs on average once every eighteen years. The failure of the ITCZ to reach Zimbabwe is the main cause of a drought. The Zimbabwe farmers look on the television-weather report with dismay when the ITCZ is graphically marked on the continent way above the country's northern border. At the time of writing, 1992, Zimbabwe is experiencing the worst drought ever recorded. Even the mighty baobab trees are shrinking. Dams lie dry everywhere, and farmers watch as their herds of livestock perish. The wildlife suffers too. Elephant cows abandon their calves, knowing that they need their strength to carry them through to the next season. Instinct tells them to survive to produce offspring in more favourable conditions. ∎

THE HOT WET SEASON

Zimbabwe's hot wet season is its summer, which runs from October through to March. During this period almost all of the country's annual rainfall occurs, and temperatures are normally between 85 and 95°F (30 and 35°C).

Late in November the rains begin in earnest. With the first substantial rainfall the bulk of the game disperses inland, leaving the resident population and the floodplain to recover from the rigours of the previous dry season.

By the time the rains come, almost all the food on the floodplain has been exhausted; the animals have been surviving on their fat reserves alone. The first flush of plants appearing in response to the temperature increase (of about 40°F [4–5°C]) together with the promise of rain offer an immediate but small hors d'oeuvre for the resident game population.

But now the time of plenty is at hand. Soon the whole landscape changes, green grass springs up side by side with the really hammered patches of ground. Miraculously, the harsh, hazy, dry days are forgotten, as the scenery changes to the clean green parkland of the floodplain.

BUSH ORCHESTRA

Frogs are calling everywhere, each male trying to make his call heard above the others' in his quest to attract a female. Many different species call in unison – the running and champagne frogs trill and plop; the sharp-nosed grass frogs ting; add to these the chirruping call of the grey tree frog, and the bush orchestra is complete.

The grey tree frogs find a branch overhanging a small or large pan of water and begin to build a nest. They secrete a substance onto their hind legs and rub it together to make a foamy solution. Into this solution they deposit their eggs. The outside of the nest hardens, retaining the moisture inside. When the eggs hatch inside, the weight of the tadpoles causes the nest to split open, releasing the tadpoles, who drop into the water below. ∎

The grey tree frog's nest overhangs a stretch of water. When the tadpoles mature they fall from the nest into the water below.

AERIAL INVASION

Insects are to be found everywhere in the bush, whether as larvae, caterpillars, or parasites – and their predators have timed their migration to arrive here the instant the banquet is ready. Many migrant sunbirds arrive as soon as the flowering plants appear in August/September. Whole flights of birds sweep in from equatorial Africa and Europe. From the tropics come woodland kingfishers, who set up their territories immediately on landing, staking their claims with vociferous trilling calls.

From Europe the swallows flock in. One bird, ringed in Africa and collected in the CIS (then the Soviet Union), was recorded having travelled 7,500 miles (12,000 kilometres) in thirty-four days (Roberts, 1940) Successive flights bring in swifts and martins, waders, tiny warblers, and the white storks. All have heroic and tragic debriefing stories to tell of overflying hidden gun emplacements manned by their arch enemy, the human hunters, who threaten the migrating flocks all along the overland stretches of their routes. ∎

Some swifts travel thousands of miles in their migration from the cold European winter. Nesting sites include palm trees, and some species use sand - or river banks.

THE APPETITE OF A LUNGFISH

The filling of the waterholes – called 'pans' locally – has brought the lungfish out of their winter hibernation. When the pans dried up the lungfish burrowed down into the mud to pass the dry season in their moist cocoons (see page 209). Now, having used up their fat reserves, their voracious appetite is at its keenest, and they will eat anything unlucky enough to have been washed into the pan with the rains. Insects, lizards, even frogs, are guzzled with gusto. A similar species of fish is the catfish, which unfortunately does not possess these survival techniques. When the rains have been heavy enough, catfish, breeding in the shallow widespread waters, make their way into the pans. As the waters recede at the season's end many are trapped, and those trapped in the pans that dry up completely will die, since they cannot hibernate like the lungfish.

This wet time of year makes game-viewing difficult. Access to the floodplain can be made only in a four-wheel drive vehicle, and often even this is not powerful enough in really wet conditions. People prefer to boat down the river and do their game-viewing on foot.

The description of the greedy lungfish (above) reminds us of a boat trip we took to Mana Pools while doing research for this book. A few of us were drifting down the river in our canoes, about twelve miles (twenty kilometres) upstream from Mana. There is nothing better than hanging around, identifying birds, putting the odd line in the water, and drinking a beer or two. Suddenly a voice shouted at us from the Zambian side of the river: 'Pamberi ne Zambia' (Forward Zambia). 'Pamberi ne Zimbabwe', Stan Fourie shouted back. Soon a verbal exchange started that would have embarrassed a sailor. We anchored and continued our attack. All of a sudden there was silence, and one of our friends on board, James Hughes, sat back contentedly, convinced we had the Zambian fisherman on the point of tears. Then a voice was heard somewhere in the reeds, 'Ah, you are nothing more than a rat's penis'! James decided that this was truly a worthy foe, and we all agreed to go and have a drink with the fellow. We found the sinewy gentleman, clad only in a pair of shorts, sitting in his dugout canoe. We handed him a bottle of brandy and reached around for a glass and some Coca-Cola. When we turned to hand him the Coca-Cola he was holding an empty bottle in his hand! ■

NATIVITY SEASON

The births of many young creatures are timed to coincide with the arrival of the rains, when food is plentiful. Baby crocodiles, now fully developed in nests beneath the sand, are making their strange calls to signal to their mother, waiting nearby, that they are hatching. She will come out of the water to dig them out, carrying many back to the river in her mouth. This is the period of greatest vulnerability for them, for many crocodile eggs are dug up and eaten by monitor lizards when the female is not in attendance. Once in the river, this danger is passed, and the newly hatched crocodiles' chances of survival seemingly increase. But they are so heavily predated upon by catfish, storks, and virtually anything that can make a meal of them, that from each batch of an average of forty eggs, it is estimated that only one per cent of young survive. ■

Water leguaans are Africa's largest lizards. They will often dig up and eat crocodile's eggs and terrapins They also feed on young water birds.

Impala young are able to run with the herd only a few days after birth. Post-natal 'imprinting', done away from the herd, means that even if separated from its mother, the calf still recognizes her smell.

The births of baby warthogs coincide with the rains. The young hoglets are endearing little creatures, and it is amusing to watch a whole family trotting off in single file, all holding their tails straight up, like a line of radio aerials mounted on the tailwings of a row of cars.

When viewed from the front, adult warthogs can be sexed by their facial warts, which are made of gristle. The male has two large pairs of warts, one by his eyes and one by his tusks. The pair by the tusks act as shock absorbers during fights; and the other pair protects the eyes. The females (as non-combatants) have only one, much-reduced pair near the eyes.

Warthogs live in holes in the ground – usually in holes made by antbears in pursuit of termites. Without these holes warthogs would be very vulnerable indeed. The holes are too narrow for their occupants to turn around in, so they always reverse into them – for two reasons: firstly, if danger threatens they can defend their holes with their formidable tusks while their heads block the entrance; and secondly, by emerging head first, they can check that the coast is clear before venturing out.

FLOODING THE MARKET

Impalas also time their flood of births to coincide with the new green flush, so that food is available to enable the mothers to produce sufficient milk for their young. For security reasons the females move away from the herds to give birth where the bush is thick. It is here that the initial 'imprinting' is done; it is vital for their survival that the young quickly recognize their mother's scent. Impala young are almost all legs when born – they need the long legs to enable them to run that little bit faster to escape predation. After a few days they join the herd, which will not have moved too far away.

Impalas are ecotonal animals (an ecotone is an area where two habitat types merge). They are therefore normally to be found on the fringes of open woodland, bordering on plains. Like all plains game they form herds, the many eyes and ears providing added security, and making each animal, as part of a large herd, less conspicuous. Predators almost always select a single animal on which to mount an attack. To give birth randomly through the year on the plains would therefore make the impala young highly visible to predators; they would be snatched up in seconds, and none would survive.

Male (left) *and female* (right) *warthogs. Adult warthogs can be sexed by the pairs of warts on their faces: the males have two and the females only one.*

The answer is to flood the market. To this end most plains game species time the bulk of their births to occur within a period of two to three weeks. That way the predators are unable to do real justice to such an abundance of easy meals, and many impala young survive.

The reverse is true for the animals that inhabit the thick bush – kudu, bushbuck, and nyala, for example. The main concentration of predators lives on the plains and the savannah (the grasslands). As it is not practical to move in a herd in thick bush, the animals roam singly, or in small family units, relying on their camouflage to conceal themselves and their young from predators. They do not need to flood the market, and can afford to have their young throughout the year, although the number of births will peak at optimum times, that is, during and just after the rains. ∎

Warthogs always run with their tails held vertical so they are visible to their young even in long grass.

It is November, early in the wet season, close to the start of the Zambezi escarpment – the hills in the background. Two kudu bulls and a cow have been drinking at one of the new streams flowing down from the escarpment. Kudu are very wary when they drink: ears high and wide, nose up, sniffing the air; they take just a couple of cautious paces forward at a time.

THE PREDATORS

A lion leaps on to a zebra at the end of a chase, digging its claws into its victim's flanks to gain a grip. The lion's weight will bring the zebra down.

Toward the end of the harsh dry months, the predators have enjoyed easy pickings from game in poor condition concentrated around the last remaining waterholes. The lionesses, stimulated by this – as they are during good conditions at any time – come into oestrus and are covered by the males. Since their gestation period is three and a half months, the litter, averaging three cubs, will normally be born during the rainy season, when the lush vegetation provides adequate cover.

Lion prides are continuously on the move, so the lionesses move away from the pride to give birth to blind and helpless cubs. The cubs are hidden in good cover when she goes hunting. It has often been observed that should all but one cub die for some reason, a lioness may lose interest in the survivor, so that dies too.

We knew of one lioness with a pair of cubs who was noticed one day pacing back and forth along the riverbank. She was giving the low mewing call that lionesses use to call their cubs. As we could see only one cub with her, we realized that a crocodile, moving with lightning speed from the river's depths, had probably snatched one unsuspecting cub. We saw the remaining cub over the next couple of weeks struggling more and more to keep up with its mother; then one day we saw it no more.

A lioness will come in oestrus again fairly shortly after losing her litter. From a species-survival point of view, it makes more sense to bring up a new litter of three than to expend the same effort rearing a single cub.

All predators can match any sudden increase in their prey populations, and none better than the lion, the only social cat. Like most predators, lions have a gestation period of less than half that of most of their prey, and will normally produce an excess of cubs. With a sudden increase in prey numbers following a very successful breeding season due to excellent rains, this excess of cubs will survive to match the prey increase. Should the season be an average one, with only a small prey increase, then most of these cubs will die, as there will not be enough food for all of them. Nature always maintains this equilibrium by weeding out all the diseased and weak individuals. This trimming of species numbers can occur during a drought. Drought conditions cause prey populations to crash, with only the strongest surviving. For the predators this is a time of easy pickings. The following season there is a huge predator population, but little prey, all of whom are in peak condition. This imbalance results in the demise of the weaker predators, who are unable to compete with their stronger counterparts. Soon the correct ratio is achieved between the species, with the survivors creating the best breeding nucleus for the populations to explode when times are right. ∎

A lioness and her young beside a wet-season pan. The vegetation around the pan provides plenty of cover for the cubs to hide in when their mother goes hunting.

PROJECT LION

It is unusual to see big territorial lions actually hunting. They normally rely on the sleeker, more agile lionesses to do the killing, and arrive only after the hunt, to join the feast. They are also quick to appropriate the kills of other predators. The male's job is to defend the pride territory from nomadic males, keeping the young safe and enabling the females to breed successfully.

This natural mechanism that keeps numbers in equilibrium was proved conclusively by a research project carried out in Kruger National Park in South Africa, and published in 1982, in a book by Dr B. Smuts, *Lion*. After monitoring a drastic decrease in the wildebeest and zebra populations in the central part of the Park, it was eventually decided to conduct a lion cull of about a thousand animals. Intensive research after the cull showed a continued decrease in the two prey species.

When ideas to explain this were almost exhausted, a change took place in the rain cycle, leading to an increase in the numbers of zebra and wildebeest. It is thought that worldwide we experience wet and dry cycles, each lasting seven to ten years. A dry cycle does not necessarily mean drought, but overall less-than-average rainfall. During a wet cycle the bush thickens; during a dry cycle it thins. Thicker bush tends to break herds down into smaller units, as it is difficult for a herd to remain in contact and in sight of each other when fleeing from danger.

Small units reduce the numbers of eyes and ears of prey on the lookout for predators, and this gives the lions far greater hunting success. With the lions producing excess cubs every season, as described above, Dr Smuts speculates that all the cull really did was remove the excess. Thus the number of hunting lions was not significantly reduced, so the prey continued to decrease in numbers. The coming dry cycle swung the whole process round. ∎

POPULATION CONTROL

HERBIVORE HIERARCHY

When the seasons are good, the herbivores increase. Come the bad times, many die. Grazing (grass-eating) herbivores overgraze the land during dry cycles. The grasses that are the most palatable to them die off, resulting in excess water run-off. They are replaced by poor, unpalatable species that are able to colonize the low-moisture soils. With little good to eat, the remaining grazers move elsewhere and the area is allowed to recover.

As a secondary means of population control, a low plane of nutrition renders the animals less able to cope with their internal parasites. These parasites build up to dangerous levels, killing off the more unhealthy hosts. It seems that ticks favour the unpalatable plant species that prevail in overgrazed conditions, and thus increase in numbers. Huge tick infestations may also cause unhealthy hosts to die through anaemia. By the end of the period of adverse conditions, only the very strongest herbivores survive – to reproduce the good genes.

By the time the wet cycle begins again, many less palatable primary species have colonized large areas, causing the bulk of the herbivores and their predators to move off, thus allowing the area to recover. These unsavory plants now bind the soil, reducing run-off; this creates wetter conditions which these same species do not enjoy. They gradually die off and are replaced by species more palatable to the grazing herbivore hierarchy. ∎

Although there is some competition among the browsing (leaf-eating) herbivores, particularly during dry cycles, the various species generally feed on different plants. When feeding on the same species of plant, they tend to feed at different heights, or on different parts of the plant. Eland reach higher than kudu, which reach slightly higher than nyala. Bushbuck occupy the next rung down the ladder, with duiker and grysbuck at the bottom.

It is still a mystery why identical habitats in different parts of Africa support different species of animals. The Luangwa National Park in Zambia, and Mana Pools National Park in Zimbabwe are a good example: in the Luangwa region there is a wildebeest and giraffe population, which the Zambezi valley lacks.

Common to both areas though, are zebras. Zebras are separated from other grazers in that they have strong lips, which push the grass between their incisors, where it is then cut. Zebra tend to feed on short young grass. Generally, grazers are not separated so much by their height, but by which part of the grass they feed on and also, to a lesser degree, by habitat.

A nyala drinking. This timid animal takes time to work its way warily down to the water.

About 8pm in early December and the plains are moonlit. A pair of kudu bulls moves out to find a feeding place. Like most herbivores, kudu operate through a 24-hour schedule, feeding for sixteen to eighteen hours, with intermittent rests, but these times can be changed drastically, either by severe food shortages or during intense harassment.

Zebras can eat top-grass stratum, the most fibrous part of the plant. Unlike ruminants, they have a single-chambered stomach, and although their digestion is not as efficient as the ruminants', their stomachs contain protozoans, which can break down the coarse fibrous tissue that ruminants are unable to utilize.

These are the reasons why you will seldom see a thin zebra when times are harsh. They also have a layer of yellow fat beneath the mane; when this energy reserve has been utilized, the mane begins to droop.

Zebra, then, are usually the last of the grazers to succumb during drought. The next in line would be wildebeest (although these are not seen around Mana Pools).

The sable antelope feed toward the bottom of the grass plant. The lower leaves, and sometimes the stalks, are eaten by impalas. Impalas have been very successful in this food-sharing system because they are the only herbivore that grazes and browses in an equal ratio throughout the year. A grazer may take in a small amount of browse normally, and vice-versa. The impala simply turns to browse when the graze runs out.

If you look still lower you might see warthogs digging down to find the corms and tubers.

This is why, on the huge East African migrations, the general pattern is that the zebra arrive first to open up the top stratum of grass. Wildebeest follow, feeding on the newly exposed central grass stem; and they in turn open up the mid-section for the gazelles coming up behind. ∎

Zebras often call when separated from the rest of the group, whose members will then answer in kind.

Warthogs kneel down to reach the tubers and bulbs of plants.

THE PANS

New pans are continually being formed in the bush. Similarly, many silt up at an early stage of development, or even when they are well established. The masters of pan-building are those wonderful engineers, the elephants. The massive bulk of their bodies causes them to sink down into the wet soil with every step, particularly in clay, each footprint a potential new pan.

When a mature tree dies, as a result of debarking by an elephant, disease, or old age, it will eventually topple over, leaving a large depression where its roots were. This is another ideal water-catchment area and a potential pan. Zebras also play a part in pan-building by dust-bathing – rolling in patches of fine clay. This creates a depression in an area that is especially good for water retention.

As new pans are being formed, so are old ones silting up. The most likely reason for this is the exhaustion of the food source in the area, so that the animals move out to greener pastures. But before a pan silts up, the many animals using it leave their droppings in and around it, thereby fertilizing it. Once the pan is silted up, the compacted clay line below it still traps water, ensuring a good soil moisture content above. This moisture, combined with the fertilizer, will sponsor a vigorous growth of grass on the surface.

Very occasionally a pan in just the right area will survive and enlarge to form a perennial pan. This microhabitat will support a whole community of creatures. ■

An elephant cow and her calf play in the mud at a pan. It is thought that elephants wallow in different pans to those in which they drink.

Stages in the formation of a pan: (1) an elephant's footprint (an elongated back foot on top of a rounded front foot); (2) the footprint has sunk in and a pool has formed in it and filled with aquatic life; (3) the warthog finds this a suitable wallowing place and so starts the deepening and widening process.

Elephants often wade into deep, well-established pans to feed on aquatic plants. This could be a deep, still backwater on the side of the Zambezi River. The bird is a jacana, attracted by the many insects found on the plants here, and can walk on the floating aquatic vegetation because its huge feet spread its weight over a wide surface area. Elephants often defecate in these waters, thus enriching the pan with ready-made fertilizer. The cows seldom venture into deep pans or backwaters to feed, as they would be very vulnerable, and unable to protect their young, who could not follow.

A typical floodplain pan makes a meeting place for three herds. In the background is a bachelor herd of impalas. Drinking at the pan is a typical family unit of zebra. And, just approaching, a small cow herd of elephants; the youngest is around two and a half years old (you can just see the tip of his tusk), and the others are roughly four years apart. Cape turtle doves are also drinking at the pan. The vegetation is plentiful. The albida trees are marked with an elephant browse line. On the surface of the pan are two types of weed: the water cabbage, pistia, and azolla, which turns maroon as the heat intensifies.

THE BENEFITS OF WALLOWING

As the rains continue, the footprint is kept topped up with water. All sorts of aquatic life quickly move in. Bacteria, algae and fungi, once established, provide food for things like insect larvae, tadpoles, and fairy shrimps. These may soon have their lives disrupted should the footprint-pan prove an ideal wallow for a warthog. Any self-respecting warthog passing during the heat of the day will always pull in and lie in the depression to have a good wallow. Animals wallow to give themselves some respite from the sun and the many biting insects that plague them. The wallowing complete, the warthog will clamber out and find a stump, or even a termite mound to use as a rubbing or scratching post. By rubbing off the drying mud it will dislodge most of the really persistent parasites. The warthog has also deepened the depression by the amount of mud that clung to its body when it got up.

Through this process happening frequently over a couple of months, the pan will eventually be deep enough for a buffalo or a rhino to wallow in, and this speeds up its formation.

Lastly, when the size is right, back comes the elephant, whose weight aids the final compaction to ensure good water retention. The elephants accelerate the pan formation process by wallowing in these new depressions.

The formation of pans begins in summer, with the rains. For the new pans to survive, they must have the best water retention of all the pans close by. When there is plenty of water around, there will be many wallowing places, and they will be used sporadically. As the dry season approaches and some dry out, the remaining ones will be used more and more. They will now quickly widen and deepen, far exceeding their competitors, which will probably dry and disappear.

With each summer, the surviving pans will enlarge to house an ever-widening variety of aquatic creatures. A large elephant population certainly speeds up the process! Researchers estimate that adult elephants remove in the region of one ton of mud from waterholes every year, by wallowing, or throwing mud on to their bodies with their trunks. ∎

A zebra dust-bathing creates a depression in which a pan may form.

Buffalo bulls move about singly, or in small, all-male groups. They move randomly in and out of breeding herds. When facing you, bulls can be identified by the big solid horn area in the middle of their forehead, known as a 'boss'. Female buffalos do not have a boss.

Mid-afternoon early in the dry season. Two buffalo are starting to feed after the noon siesta and a wallow in the dagga (thick mud). They are trying to get at the grass growing under a fallen acacia tree that died after elephants debarked it. The thorns of the dying acacia protected the grass seeds beneath them, so they were able to germinate. The elephant dung in front of the termite mound acts as a natural compost for any seeds that may be contained within it.

FOLLOW-ME SIGNS

The side-striped jackal hunts mostly at night. This dog-like animal survives on a diet of vegetable matter, small game and, of course, carrion.

Animals have their various colorations and markings for good reasons. One is obviously camouflage. Some of the more intricate markings also act as what are called `follow-me signs'. Researchers believe that all mammals except the primates see in black and white. The reason they put forward to explain this lies in the number of rods and cones in the retina, the layer of light-sensitive cells at the back of the eye. The ratio of rods to cones in the retinas of different creatures determines how well they see in the dark. Rods are sensitive to light, but not to colour. Cones are the colour-sensitive cells in the retina, and different cone cells are sensitive to different wavelengths of light, so the numbers and types of cone cells in the retina dictate whether a creature can see colour, and which colours it can see.

The majority of mammals have a far greater concentration of rods than humans, which is why our night vision is limited and theirs is excellent. We, on the other hand, have a far greater concentration of cones so we have better colour vision.

Most mammals' follow-me signs are, therefore, either black or white, both of which stand out effectively against a grey background. The purpose of follow-me signs is to ensure that animals stay with each other when fleeing. An individual separated from a herd will almost always be set upon by predators.

Impala have black stripes down their rumps, but for displays they lift up their white tails. Waterbuck have a big white ring on their rear ends. Zebra may look very conspicuous close up on the open plain, but when they are further away, their black-and-white stripes merge to form grey, the ideal camouflage in a grey background. In woodland, their vertical stripes blend in with the vertical trees and shrubs. Yet if they turn to run away they suddenly become much more visible, because the stripes on their rumps are horizontal – a perfect follow-me sign in the vertical surroundings.

It would be impractical for warthogs to have a sign on their rumps. Because they are short, if chased by a predator into fairly long grass, they could not see such a sign in front of them. So warthogs raise their tails high as they run. They look very comical, but that little aerial with the tassel on the top stands out well. Buffalo are big and black, and are therefore very noticeable in flight. Elephant and rhinoceros never developed follow-me signs, because their eyesight is poor. As a natural defence their young always remain close to their parents. Unfortunately, since the invention of the gun, man has become a real threat to their existence.

Among the predators, lions are well camouflaged, looked at front on, as their prey would see them. But the black tips behind their ears are very conspicuous, enabling pride members from behind to see what the ones in front are doing. The black tips on their tails also give the cubs something to watch when following the adults. Leopards have black and white behind the ears, and white tips on their tails for the same reasons as lions. ∎

Follow-me signs come in many shapes and sizes. They are at the rear of the animal, and are always either black or white. Shown here: the zebra has vertical lines at the rear of its body; the leopard (top left) has a white tip on its tail; the waterbuck (top right) has a white 'toilet-seat' effect; the impala (bottom right) has a white tip on its tail; and the lion (bottom left) has a black tip on its tail.

Two kudu cows drink at a pan in the midday heat. The vertical stripes on their backs help break up their outline in the bush - making them blend into the shadows behind them. The hindmost cow has its ears up, and a black sock, indicating that she took a step forward into the pan, but then heard a sound and drew back. The kudu's big ears give excellent hearing.

OTHER ANTI-PREDATOR DEVICES

This lion may die from its wounds. Being fairly barbed, porcupine quills remain embedded in the skin and can work their way in more deeply.

As well as camouflage, prey adopt a variety of anti-predator behaviour to confuse their predators. Impalas, if attacked, leap explosively in different directions, and continue to leap every couple of strides as they run away, making it more difficult for the predator to lock on to its selected individual. The predator has to pause only for a split second, and the prey will make good its escape. As kudu burst away, lifting up their tails, their white undersides suddenly flash. When many do this at once, they create a similar effect to the impalas.

Zebras, when attacked out on the open plains bunch closely together to form a mass of black-and-white stripes, making it difficult for an individual to be selected. Buffalo form a tight bunch if unable to escape easily, with the adults facing the threat. Baboon males rush to the source of the threat while the females gather all the young together.

When attacked, baboons will run down from the trees. Monkeys, if on the ground, run up the

Porcupines reverse into their attackers. When their quills make contact, they are able to detach them easily to leave them in the attacker, where they may cause serious, even fatal infection.

The pangolin, or scaly anteater, is a shy, secretive creature and seldom seen, due to its nocturnal habits. Its scales are a form of armour-plating. This one is looking for termites, on which it feeds. The pangolin is traditionally a gift given to African tribal chiefs by subordinates.

trees. Baboons, being large creatures, can best defend themselves as a group, and take to the trees only if separated. Monkeys, by contrast, are small, and extremely fleet-footed and agile. By foraging in smaller groups they are better able to escape any threat from the canopy. The bush squirrels live mostly in the holes in the mopane trunks, which is why they are also called mopane squirrels. They always seem to be on the wrong side of the road, and have to dash in front of your vehicle, just making it with inches to spare. They act as excellent alarms for the community of the mopanes, as they hurl abuse at any predator who may pass through. When birds of prey fly by, their chattering creates an almost stereophonic effect. The calls start off faintly on one side, reach a peak, and then fade into the distance, making it easy to locate the area of the bird of prey.

The midday heat is truce-time, when both hunter and hunted drop their guards and rest. If there is a good canopy overhead, walking at midday – when it is cool enough – can be rewarding. You can sneak far closer to the animals than at any other time of the day, and still remain undetected. ∎

Kudu can clear a seven-foot (two-metre) fence from a standing position quite effortlessly. At a run they can clear a ten-foot (three-metre) obstacle.

The striped skink is famous for its survival strategy. If a predator grabs its middle section, the tail half of the creature breaks off, and continues twitching to attract the assailant's attention, while the rest of the skink makes off to safety.

It is rare for kudu to be unable to extricate themselves after interlocking horns whilst fighting, but it has been recorded.

*A male cheetah lying in long grass, his
colours blending in perfectly with his
surroundings. Males have a stockier
appearance than females, and larger, more
square-shaped heads.*

Savannah country – open woodland – a female leopard has returned with an impala for her cubs. Leopards will normally drag a kill to safety up a tree, where it cannot be taken by hyenas or vultures. This, however, might be a lesson in feeding – introducing the cubs to the kill. Zebras, curious, keep a safe distance between themselves and these predators.

The occasional flash of wings in the darkness betrays the arrival of the pennant-winged nightjar from the northern tropics. The males grow long pennants as breeding plumage, and it is these we glimpse as he makes his way through the night in pursuit of the last of the alates (winged termites).

THE NUPTIAL FLIGHT OF THE TERMITES

This steppe eagle does not specifically feed on termite alates, but is often seen on the ground feeding on them as they emerge from within the termite mound.

Between November and early December, winged termites or, alates, are released from the termitarium via breeches (openings) specially prepared for the occasion. These breeches are only unsealed at the approach of the alates, and then only with the support of many soldiers. This is in order to reduce to a minimum the possible invasion of their arch enemies, the matabele ants.

Unlike the worker termites, the alates are all fertile and destined to become the future kings and queens of the new colonies they plan to set up after their dispersal from the terminarium. The workers breech the escape routes, and the alates pour into the heavens. Unfortunately, many are eaten by a host of predators as they emerge, and numerous others are caught in flight. Cashing in on this feast are bushpigs, reptiles, birds, humans and many other species. This protein banquet is not just a great delicacy, but a godsend to many creatures in the process of recovery from the harsh dry season. However, the sheer explosion of numbers wins out, and a good many termites survive this onslaught.

The nuptial flight of the alates normally takes place from just before sunset to early evening, but it may occur at any time during cloudy overcast or rainy conditions.

After a short flight, the alates land. The females immediately point their abdomens skyward and release a pheromone (a scent that is irresistible to the males), which they fan into the air with their wings (which they then shed, if not already done on landing). The males shed their wings on landing, as they are now useless and a hindrance to them in their pursuit of a mate. Having paired, the alates rush away nose to tail, the female in front, in search of a new home. On finding a suitable location, they dig down, hollow out a chamber, and mate. The new queen begins laying eggs quite soon after mating has taken place, one or two eggs at a time initially, but building up to approximately 25,000 eggs per day.

Many workers are produced initially, along with a smaller percentage of soldiers for security; both are sterile – males and females. Amazingly, once the termitarium is established, messages are passed around the colony with reference to its requirements, through pheromones thought to be passed in the saliva through individual contact. If many soldiers are killed in a battle with ants, the news will reach the queen via pheromone messages, and her next batch of eggs will turn into predominantly soldiers. Science is unsure as to whether this is brought about in some way by the queen, or whether it is due to the type of food fed to the nymphs. ∎

The slender mongoose is one of three common types of mongoose found in the Zambezi valley. Unlike the banded and dwarf mongooses, this one roams alone, or in pairs, and its diet differs in that it eats snakes, rodents, and will raid bird nests, while its cousins remain insectivorous.

THE HEAT SETS IN

INSECT INVASION

By the end of December the impala lambs have grown big enough to no longer make easy meals for predators, and the predators have now reached a time when they have to work much harder to catch their food. The dispersal of the prey with the onset of the rains (*see* page 26) means a smaller concentration of prey in the area, and in addition, the thickening of the bush has made it much more difficult to locate them. It is now hot, with a high level of humidity, created not only by the abundance of water, but also by transpiration from the lush wet undergrowth. ■

The setting in of the rains is heralded by the emergence of huge numbers of insects of all shapes, sizes and colours, and they seem to be everywhere, sometimes making life very uncomfortable. Depending on the conditions prevailing in the previous season, there will be an over-abundance of one species or another that favoured such conditions. One year it was little black stinkbugs, which managed to be everywhere they were not wanted, releasing their pungent smell – often inadvertently in our cooking pot when they fell in.

Another time it was ground crickets. Close up, these look like something out of a horror movie. They are scavengers, and are not above eating one of their own kind that has been crushed underfoot. Some complain bitterly if so much as prodded lightly, while others – the rugged ones – make their high-pitched squeaking sound only under great duress (rather like people, in a way!). You quickly become used to their presence, however, and in no time at all they can even endear themselves to you. Until, that is, you have to remove one from under the lavatory seat after it has tickled your rear with its feelers, and taken another out of your shoe. They even find their way through your mosquito net into your bed at night. ■

The ground crickets are in evidence only during the summer, and do not sing, but make a harsher version of the normal cricket noise.

A pair of guinea fowl. The one ahead is dusting itself to help remove parasites. Guinea fowl pair off shortly after the rains have set in, in preparation for breeding.

UNDERSTANDING SNAKES AND SCORPIONS

Scorpions and snakes are very much in evidence during the wet season, and their presence is readily felt as they seek places of refuge. Many people have learned the hard way to check their shoes before putting them on first thing in the morning. Scorpions are attracted to rooms by the insects they follow. These, in turn, are attracted by the light.

Snakes have a different reason for their unwelcome presence, in that they seek warmth and cover, as well as the rodents that live inside. Snakes are seldom aggressive and with some gentle persuasion may easily be moved outside.

One common intruder is the brown house snake. This little creature often feels like river sand at the end of one's takkie (a type of gym shoe used for walking in the bush). These are fantastic little snakes, which you can handle a very short time after encountering them. Even the dangerous snakes just want to escape; people are normally bitten only on provoking them. One can occasionally encounter spitting cobras and black mambas, often at close range, and they always slither away into their retreats nearby. Puff adders are reluctant to move, but rather rely on their excellent camouflage in the grass or dry leaves. Should you walk through thick grass or litter – their habitat – and encounter one, they will try to warn off the intruder at close range with their puffs.

Snakes are wonderful creatures, only despised through ignorance, dramatized stories and, of course, as a result of forgetting that any harmful incidents are rare. A rural doctor, looking after a population of thousands of people, many of whom wander around the bush barefoot, told us that he deals with only about six snake-bite victims a year. If snakes were largely eradicated there would be an accompanying explosion of rodents, and corresponding human diseases.

Besides pythons, who constrict their prey, snakes can be divided into front- and back-fanged species. The back-fanged varieties are relatively unaggressive and, because their fangs are set far back in their mouths, they have to really bite to puncture your skin. When they do, therefore, often very little venom is injected. Front-fanged snakes, like the cobras, adders and mambas, inject venom more easily; black mambas also bite many times in quick succession, and are regarded as a very quick and dangerous snake.

Venom is not necessarily injected after a snake-bite, and victims should not panic after a strike, because only the tiniest percentage of bites proves to be fatal.

It is most important to know your snakes; many harmless and beautiful snakes are unceremoniously pummelled to death because of man's ignorance and fear. ■

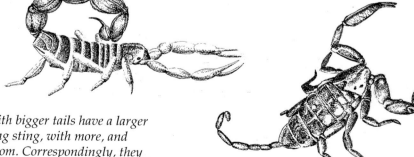

A boomslang ingesting a chameleon. This snake is back-fanged and reluctant to strike at people. Because of this reticence, it was many years before people realized that the boomslang is in fact a very dangerous snake!

Striped field mice are numerous in the vetiveria, providing a good food source for many small predators.

Scorpions with bigger tails have a larger accompanying sting, with more, and stronger venom. Correspondingly, they also have smaller pincers, as the venom does most of the subduing.

IN PRAISE OF CREEPY-CRAWLIES

THE SOUND OF SILENCE

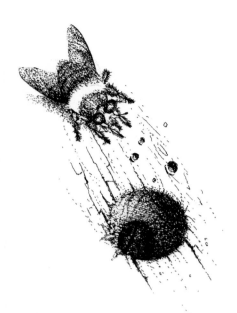

A robber fly lying in ambush, alert for the signal to scramble, and to intercept other flying insects.

A baboon spider with its two front legs raised in a defence posture. The hairiness of its legs and the baboon-like underfoot explain its strange name.

Mantises do not turn the colour of the leaf they are on, as some people believe, but are born that colour and thus remain on that type of tree.

Again, simply through ignorance, many people are revolted by creepy-crawlies, yet if you are prepared to hear about them it is easy to become hooked on this fascinating world. When there is a shortage of large mammals, especially during the wet season, these small creatures seem to be everywhere.

A fearsome-looking insect to find in your room is the solifuge, or rain spider, which, as the name suggests, comes out of hibernation just at the onset of the rains. Rain spiders have their own family within the Arachnidae. They are orangey in colour, with many fine hairs all over their body. They are armed with two sets of jaws that move vertically, and usually crush the insects they feed on. They are harmless, but when they run into a room, dashing around with great speed searching out prey, and climbing up chairs and even low walls, it is difficult to be convinced. ∎

The December heat and humidity is not conducive to much activity beyond the early morning and late afternoon. Yet there is always something to see. Although there may be few large animals around, you can be almost certain that something – be it an elephant, a buffalo, or a tiny bushbuck, will pay you a visit. There are also plenty of insects around, and some of their behaviour is amazing. People who visit the bush seem to think that the more you drive around, the more you will see, but this is not always the case. Besides, the noise of an engine cuts out the sounds of the bush and, above all, its tranquillity.

A friend who was once entertaining some Japanese business colleagues became really frustrated when nothing his guests saw in the National Park seemed to impress them. When one of them asked him to stop the car, then just stood outside the vehicle for several minutes, he became convinced that he must be doing something wrong. Worried, he eventually asked the man's colleagues, who had remained in the car, what the problem was. `There is no problem,' they replied; `our friend has never heard silence before.' ∎

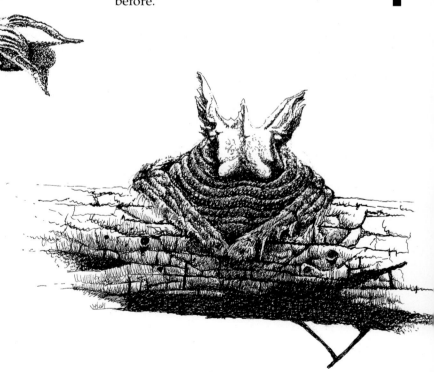

A bark spider mimicking a knot on a branch. An experienced eye is needed to penetrate its disguise.

INSECT MIMICS

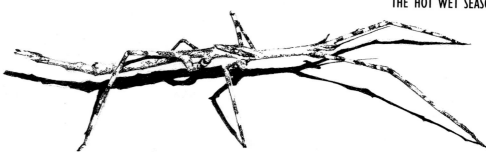

During many days spent quietly at water-holes we often see robber flies, one of the many insect predators, intercepting other flying insects. It can be almost as exciting as watching a lion pulling down a zebra, crashing to the ground, locked in combat. Attacking just as effectively as a lion, but on a much smaller scale, the robber fly is a top-class predator. The robber fly is able to hold on with the aid of its barbed legs, and make good its kill with its sharp proboscis.

Robber flies belong to the family Asilidae. The asilids are notorious for their mimicry, many species mimicking their prey almost exactly. If you see a friendly black-and-white carpenter bee sitting motionless on a twig, when you know it should normally be active, look twice at the mouthparts and you are more than likely to find that it is an asilid impostor, called a hyperechia. Another asilid mimic, proagonistes, preys on the pompilid wasp, which in turn preys on the baboon spider. All asilids though, have a slightly different stance and head shape to the insects that they mimic.

It must be remembered that not every mimic is an asilid. Many other insects have excellent camouflages. We once saw a preying mantis that had become, to all intents and purposes, a small pink flower. We only penetrated its disguise when one of our guests bent down to look more closely at it, and the flower jumped.

There are grasshoppers who so resemble a little bit of green grass protruding from the soil that the only way you will spot one is when it jumps. During Zimbabwe's current drought conditions (1992) it is easy to imagine the goats, of whom it is said that they are so desperate for nourishment that they could eat the traffic lights when they turn green, chasing after these jumping grasses!

SPIDERS' DISGUISES

Spiders also adopt some sleazy outfits. Flower spiders hide among the petals of flowers whose colours they imitate, then ambush the various insects visiting the flower. Some spiders even mimic ants, and a common experience with members of the Myrmarachne family occurs when an ant is idly flicked off one's body, only to continue hanging off you, still attached by a thread. Ants mimicking spiders look like half-inch-long black ants, but have much larger jaws. Their mimicry is a way of avoiding predation by

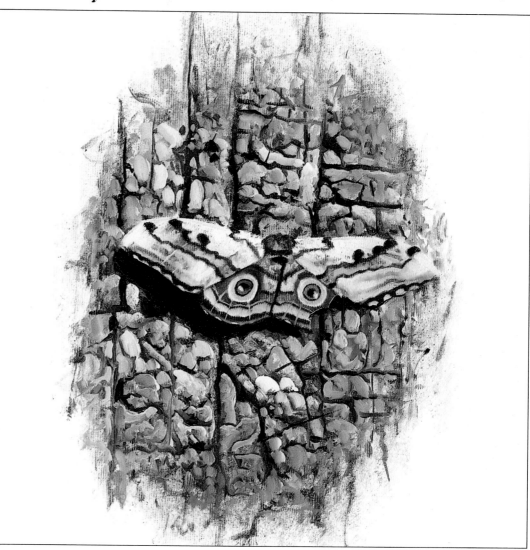

their dreaded enemies, the spider-hunting wasps, who paralyse them with their sting then feed them, live, to their larvae.

Baboon spiders are so called because the bases of their legs resemble baboons' feet. Being large and hairy, they are also often called tarantulas, but there are no true tarantulas native to Africa. The large pompilid wasps prey on them. Their battles are characterized by much parrying and countering, and the spider is normally the loser. If it can, the spider will escape the threat by disappearing down its burrow. The trapdoor spider goes further, actually making a trapdoor on the outside surface of its burrow. When it closes the door behind it, the burrow is almost impossible to find, so well-camouflaged is the trapdoor.

Another means of escape from detection is good camouflage, as with the albida moth, here blending in perfectly with its surroundings.

(top)
An eight-inch (20 cm) giant stick insect can mimic an acacia branch so well that its body even has protruding mock thorns, resembling in detail those of the acacia.

MASTERS OF DISGUISE

This caterpillar is covered with minute cocoons which produce the mature wasps.

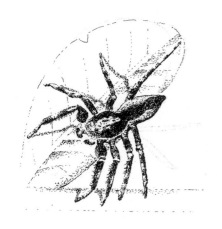

Jumping spiders do not use muscles, but a kind of jet propulsion to give the impression of jumping. They must be the most endearing of all spiders, and not even the most rabid of spider-haters could dislike them!

The caerostris, or bark spider, avoids the many parasitic wasps that prey on it by weaving a new web each night after sunset, when its predators are asleep. When its predators are active the following day, its web has already disappeared and the spider has crawled onto a branch. Once there it retracts its legs and, literally, become a node on the branch. The spider normally breaks down the web as the sky starts to lighten, but if there has been rain or a strong dew she may make a late start.

One such spider we watched chopped her guy lines, then ingested her limp web, probably with the aid of digestive enzymes, leaving behind only her bridge line for the next web. She scrambled onto the branch to which the bridge line was attached, and her transition to 'node mode' was so swift that she disappeared before our eyes.

Over the next week it became our standard practice to spend sunset near the site of her web and watch her suddenly appear as darkness fell, running across her bridge line to what was to become the centre of her web, and begin the laborious process of spinning a new one. First she would let herself down on a thread and attach her guy lines to some stable object on the ground. This done, she would begin on the orb, starting with a large circle of silk, then spinning circles of ever-decreasing diameter, until she ended up in the middle.

If we touched her at any time while she was waiting in her web, she would scramble with some speed up along the bridge line and on to the branch. Once she reached her favourite spot, she quickly reverted to node mode. Then we could touch and even push her gently, and she would not budge. She must have known instinctively that if she moved she would betray her camouflage. ∎

On another occasion we were seated by a pan in the welcome shade of a tamarind tree. Many wasp species were active, some collecting mud from the edges of the pan for building the nests. Others were busy hunting for caterpillars or jumping spiders to feed their larvae. I always feel sorry for the jumping spiders, as they seem to have such intelligent little faces; they will even jump on to your offered finger.

After watching many wasps struggling manfully past with their victims in tow, we decided to follow one and see exactly what happened. How worthwhile this proved to be! This particular wasp laboriously hauled a large caterpillar back to her hole. She had covered up the hole earlier, but had no trouble at all in relocating it. As if she was opening all the locks to her front door, she proceeded to uncover the hole, seeming all the time to complain bitterly to herself: this was not a safe neighbourhood. Her legs moved so fast in shifting the fine sand that they became invisible. Then the caterpillar was unceremoniously forced down the hole and the wasp followed to lay her egg on top.

After a couple of seconds she reappeared and began the precise task of covering up her hole. First, a flurry of legs as she loaded in fine sand. Then some larger grains of sand were placed with great precision and workmanship. These were rearranged a couple of times, and one that did not fit exactly was discarded. Then more fine sand, some coarse sand, and so on, until the hole was covered level with the surface. Now came the amazing part. This, she decided, was not good enough, so she camouflaged the area. First she scattered leaves and small twigs randomly around, then some pebbles. Then she decided she had overdone it and removed a couple of leaves and twigs.

This so impressed us, that when a spider-hunting wasp came past with a cricket, an unusual quarry, we could not resist following again. The cricket was too heavy for the wasp to get airborne, but nonetheless she tried over and over again, gaining about a foot with each attempt. Eventually, after she had struggled about nine feet (three metres) past a small tree, she paused as though reassessing the situation. Then, retracing her steps to the base of the tree, she climbed a little way up, dragging the cricket with her. From this new height she launched herself into the air, and managed to build up enough airspeed to keep herself airborne. ∎

ORIENTATION EXERCISES

PARASITES AND HYPERPARASITES

Scientists have long been baffled at the way insects relocate their holes and other places so exactly. One group tried an experiment on a wasp by waiting until she left her hole to search for more prey, then camouflaged the area by scuffing the ground and adding some more pebbles and leaves. On her return she paused only briefly before going unerringly to the hole and uncovering it.

We made a similar experiment with a spider called hersilia, which, we had read, was reputed to be able to return to the exact same place after it had been disturbed. Using much skill and cunning, we managed to mark with a pencil the points covered by the ends of her legs while she was stationary. We then chased her a couple of yards away, and true enough, she returned some five minutes later and placed herself exactly within the pencil marks. A second time we chased her a good fifteen feet (five metres) away, and, although it took her a few hours, we found her back in position. Researchers have even scrubbed an area after disturbing the spider, to eliminate any possibility of her returning to a scent, yet she always returns. How, we wonder, can this curious behaviour possibly benefit her? ■

A caterpillar in hair curlers is a curious sight – so much so that the one we saw definitely warranted a closer inspection. It struggled feebly and was obviously about to die. The hair curlers were minute cocoons attached to its body, and they were spun by the pupating larvae of a braconid wasp. These little wasps lay their eggs inside the body of a caterpillar by means of their ovipositor (an egg-laying device that extends from the abdomen). The larvae hatch and immediately begin to feed on the caterpillar from inside, carefully avoiding any of their host's vital organs. How nature has equipped them with this instinctive knowledge is a mystery. It seems that the larvae time their pupation to end just as their host is on its last legs, then they burst out of its sides and spin their cocoons.

But it is not all plain sailing for these parasites. They too have their parasites, known as hyperparasites. These will lay their eggs in the cocoons of the braconids, and their larvae will eat the braconid pupae. ■

This pompilid wasp paralyses her spider victim before carting it away to act as a host for her larvae.

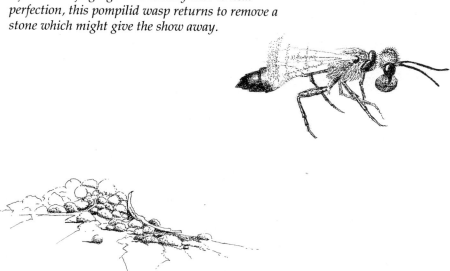

After camouflaging her hideaway nest to near-perfection, this pompilid wasp returns to remove a stone which might give the show away.

In early December the inland pans are
usually full and the surrounding area
waterlogged. Yellow-billed storks are
feeding on the numerous drowned insects.
Many geese, including egyptian and spur-
wing geese, are busy grazing on the new
blades of grass. The Zambian escarpment
is visible in the distance.

BUTTERFLIES

Flowers attract not only sunbirds (*see* page 61) but also a wealth of butterflies, many of which are resident. The blue-and-yellow pansies display their colours in flight; yet on landing they may fan their wings once or twice as a further display, and then hold them closed. In this mode they resemble the leaves they have settled among. Common grass yellows, scarlet tips, acreas and swallowtails all add flashes of colour wherever you look. Then there are the more subdued guinea fowl butterflies, cabbage whites, brown-veined whites, and commodores.

The little african monarchs fly around without fear of predation, except from ignorant birds, for they are unpalatable, and most birds recognize their black-and-orange coloration. Many palatable species, such as mimacreas and diadems, mimic these colours and benefit from a virtually predator-free existence. ■

The african monarch moves about with relative freedom in a hostile environment, as it proves most distasteful to predators.

The bee eaters' beautiful coloration makes these birds unmistakeable. The carmine (crimson) bee eater is a migratory bird, while its cousin, the little bee eater, is a year-round resident.

BIRDS

BIRD PARTIES

The scarlet-chested sunbird is not only attracted to flowers, but also includes spiders and caterpillars in its diet. The white-bellied sunbird favours nectar, though he too eats spiders and insects.

You can hardly miss the activities of the various bee eaters. Their striking colours often catch our attention as they dart here and there in pursuit of some insect. As the family name suggests, some eat bees, but not all. The little bee eater, the smallest of the family, lives up to the family name. It hunts from a perch, usually on a shrub, hawking insects with incredible agility. You can hear them from some distance away as they beat bees and wasps into submission by holding them in their bills and banging them on a branch. Their flying skills are ably matched by their slightly larger cousins, the white-fronted bee eaters. These birds share the same habitat type, but not generally the same food, preferring honey bees.

The carmine bee eaters, the largest of the family, catch much larger prey, including dragonflies. Unlike the two already described, they are migrants who do a circular migration, remaining south of the equator.

Blue-cheeked bee eaters come from Europe to Mana Pools during our summer months, but not to breed. They avoid competing with the others by feeding mostly on the wing, a lot higher up, and often over the Zambezi river. We occasionally see the small swallow-tailed bee eater, which is not as common as the others. It is about the same size as the little bee eater, but occupies a different habitat type.

On the plains, many wide, shallow pans have formed, attracting many species of stork to the drowned insects found there. Yellow-billed, woolly-necked, and open-billed storks are joined by the spur-wing and egyptian geese grazing on the fresh green shoots.

The yellow-spotted nicator, the thrush nightingale, and the bearded robin are all very secretive birds, spending much of their time in the riverine forest and the thick jesse. They make up for their shyness by their incredibly beautiful songs, and by January all three are in full swing. Although the thrush nightingale sings from deep within the thicket, the nicator and the bearded robin fly to the treetops to display and sing.

But these songs are just a small part of the many melodies played outside the immediate areas of thicket. African golden orioles and the less common European golden orioles – a lovely black on golden-yellow in colour – have soft, almost liquid calls. ∎

A bird party is a group of many species of birds, many of which feed at different levels within the canopy, or feed on different types of food. Included in these parties would be chinspot batises, puffback shrikes and crombecs. They move together as a group, and as they do so, some individuals scare food sources up or down the canopy. The creatures they do not feed on may be caught by another bird in the party. In this way they benefit each other and, as a group, have many eyes to seek out predators waiting in hiding for them.

Willow warblers are commonly heard singing as they comb their way through the albidas. Bleating warblers, their resident cousins, are breeding. The males make themselves very visible as they proclaim their territories noisily from the tops of thickets.

The sunbirds are still in a feeding frenzy. As well as the trees that have flowered, there are also many plants in flower. The plentiful food attracts the purple-banded and the collared sunbirds to join the resident species temporarily. They will move out when the cool, dryer weather comes at the end of the season. ∎

The african golden oriole is more often heard than seen. Despite its rich colouring, this bird is difficult to spot because of the thick bush in which it lives.

This overcast January day sees the waterbuck running through the water from one island to another. The calves running after the herd keep sight of the white follow-me marks on the adults' *rears. The bachelors in the foreground have been expelled from the herd, as they may compete with the bull for his females.*

THE RAINS

HIPPOS

The rains, once set in, follow an almost predictable pattern. There is always a gradual increase in temperature, leading to a build-up of cloud as a new weather system is pulled in. This intensifies, and there may be thunderstorms and lightning at night, with continual rain in the morning, lasting to about 10am. The cloud reluctantly clears during the heat of the day, building up to thunderstorms lasting, once more, into the night.

This system is known as the inter-tropical convergence zone (ITCZ); it is caused by the convergence of the north-east and south-east trade winds. If the ITCZ is not in force and the winds are moist, there may be a build-up of rain which gives thunderstorms only in the afternoon. These take the form of twenty-minute showers, then the skies clear by nightfall. There follows a spell of sunshine and the temperature build-up recurs, bringing in the moist weather again.

This is the normal seasonal pattern, but at the time of writing (1992) Zimbabwe is suffering the most severe drought in living memory, and the seasons have been generally sub-standard. In the Zambezi valley, all the rivers feeding the Zambezi are strictly seasonal, and many flow only after good rains. ∎

A hippo pod sunbathing on a sandbank beside the Zambezi. Though they secrete an oily substance from their sebaceous glands to protect their skins, they cannot remain exposed to the sun for long periods, as their skin cracks. Hippos never sunbathe very far away from the water so that they can be in it within seconds at the slightest alarm.

This lone hippo bull helps stir up the sediments at the bottom of the pan, and thus make them available to other microorganisms higher up in the water stratum. The dung excreted into the water also adds nutrients to the system.

At this time of year the hippos probably need to travel only a quarter of the distance they were travelling during the dry season, now that there is a substantial amount of grass available. They are highly gregarious, living in 'pods' averaging fifteen animals. It seems, however, that they have frequent squabbles, and all the adults bear scars as proof of this. The bulls, who fight most frequently, may be scarred all over their bodies.

The bulls hold a territory in the water, which they advertise locally, and this territory spills over on to the land. Each pod uses a number of entry and exit paths. The dominant male marks these paths by defecating on clumps of grass and shubs, and flaps his short tail while excreting to spread the dung over a wider area. Heaven help anybody reincarnated as a shrub on the edge of a hippo trail! Their paths are distinctive, with a ridge in the middle, and may travel some distance inland.

The subordinate bulls are expelled from the pods, and will often be found during the day sleeping a hundred yards or so beyond the pod. During hard times they may be forced right out of the river by pressure from the other pod males, and move into the inland pans. This benefits the pans, as the hippos' droppings bring nutrients to them; and the animals stir up sediments so that they become available to other organisms. The hippos also help to spread the seeds of aquatic plants, these seeds being carried from the river to the pans.

After a fight they have long, raking wounds all over their bodies, and it looks as though they are on their last legs. They wear an expression befitting their situation, as if the bottom has fallen out of their world, but they quickly recover. They have a layer of fat beneath that thick skin, so the wounds are only superficial. Occasionally, however, deeper wounds lead to the death of an individual.

Hippos sometimes have a full-out battle on land, or in water, and, being nocturnal animals, these almost always occur at night. By reading the story the following morning in the spoor, and by all the blood and gore, you can tell that some fights last at least a couple of hours. These clashes may prove to be fatal, as the combatants succumb to the terrible wounds inflicted.

At sunset the pod is thinking about moving up on to the banks to graze. On land it splits up into family units, each going its own way.

The hippo with cut flanks would have received its wounds from a fight with another hippo, most frequently from a territorial battle. Though the wounds often look horrific, and you wonder if the individual will survive, the wounds are usually only subcutaneous. Hippos have a thick layer of fat beneath the skin. Within a week or two the wounds heal up, and the only loss to the hippo is that of his pride!

Hippo on the Zambezi bottom. Hippos can run along the bottom of the rivers and pans, following paths that lead to their feeding grounds on land. Various people have recorded them staying under water for anything between five and eight minutes before coming up for a breath.

Hippos are in their element during the wet season – lots of green grass right on their doorstep. Young hippo calves are unable to walk far in search of grazing, so this is the peak calving period.

CROCODILES

Crocodiles are thought to open their jaws to help cool themselves - and perhaps as a way of relaxing.

Hippos seem to feed in spells through the night, resting in the sand before venturing back into the water at first light. They love to sunbathe on the islands in the midday heat, and if they are not being persecuted, they will venture out for a snack at midday. They can stay out of the water for only limited periods, because although they secrete an oily substance, their skins are sensitive to the sun. When they travel to new water sources many miles away, they therefore move mostly at night.

Hippos calve through the summer after a gestation period of eight months – surprisingly short for such a large animals, when you consider the seventeen-month gestation period of black rhino, and the nineteen-month period of white rhino. Their births peak in January. They calve so late in the season because only by then is there enough thick grass for them to feed on close by. Thus they do not have to travel far on land with their young.

Births have been recorded both on land and in the water. The cow moves out of the pod to give birth, and, like most herd animals, will stay away for two days to two weeks for the calf to imprint on her. This is the critical time, and the mother can ill afford to leave her offspring unattended for any length of time due to the ever-present danger of crocodiles. Somehow, a few calves still get lost or separated from their mothers, and will even approach our canoes in the hope of finding a foster mother. This is pitiful to see, knowing what their end will be, and being helpless to do anything for them but to leave them to their fate. ■

Hippos yawn for the same reasons as we do, but also to display their tusks to any potential rival, and to dissuade any subordinate tempted to make a challenge. Doubt exists as to whether birds feed in their mouths, as reported in North Africa.

It is not uncommon for lions to kill hippo; on these occasions the victim is normally a sub-adult, or a youngster separated from its mother. Lions readily scavenge dead hippo when the carcasses drift to the side of the river. When this happens there is often fierce competition between lions and crocodiles for the spoils.

Crocodiles and hippos share what might be best described as an uneasy truce. They may often be seen on the same sandbank. Crocodiles are largely nocturnal, although, being opportunists, they are quick to take advantage of any chance to feed. It is estimated that ninety per cent of their diet consists of fish, but the bigger the crocodile the more partial it will be to taking larger prey. The effort involved in catching a small morsel makes it uneconomical to do so.

The bigger crocodiles will often pull an impala into the river or a waterhole, after ambushing it as it drinks. Crocodiles need to be in water deeper than the height of their prey, to enable them to drown it. We have on occasions watched crocodiles chasing after buffalo as they swim from one island to the next. This would be a major battle on land, where the buffalo would have some purchase. However, in deeper water the odds turn strongly in favour of the croc.

The bigger crocodiles may just rip parts off small prey, but on larger prey they twist chunks of flesh off the carcass by spinning it around. When this occurs, a calm, innocent-looking area of water may soon transform into a writhing mass of crocodiles. A colleague of ours once counted over fifty crocodiles feeding off a carcass, which reveals just how many there are hidden within an area. One good counting system is to pan an area with a spotlight, when the red tell-tale 'brake lights' (crocodile eyes) betray their true numbers.

Crocodiles can also be very aggressive. Our colleagues once watched a pride of lions who had found a hippo carcass that had drifted to

During heavy rains catfish can move
across surface water overland, and make
their way into the pans, here to remain
throughout the summer. They will be
trapped here during the dry season, and if
the pans dry up completely they will die.
Their main predators are crocodiles.

CATFISH CONTROL

the side of the river. The lions had dragged it about 15 feet (five metres) on to the bank and were busy feeding on it. When our colleague returned after lunch a new drama was unfolding. The crocs had rallied into a formidable force, and the lions in their riot gear watched as the mob gained courage and hurled threats and abuse at the lions from their side of the carcass. There was much growling and hissing in the ensuing battle, but with the carcass next to the water, the crocs eventually won out. The carcass was finally dragged back into the water, the lions following for some distance along the bank, roaring their disapproval.

The female crocodile lays on average thirty to forty eggs in a hole she has dug in the sand on the side of the river. In the Zambezi valley this occurs in September and October, and the youngsters are normally hatched toward the end of November and the beginning of December. The temperature of the sand determines the sexes of baby crocodiles inside the eggs. Cooler temperatures produce females, and hotter temperatures males. ■

Crocodiles play an important part in the river's ecology. They help to control catfish, which are scavengers and will eat anything that they can fit in their mouths. Although these fish are indeed beneficial in keeping the river clean, they can become detrimental to the system, if they overpopulate a river or pan. By the 1950s crocodiles had been hunted almost to extinction on many of Zimbabwe's major river systems, with a consequent increase in the catfish populations.

As an example of how fragile a system may be, in some places at that time, the catfish populations were so large that they hammered the bream population by eating the eggs as well as the fry. Some of the bream species feed on aquatic vegetation, and so keep the weed in the quieter areas of water in trim. Soon there were not enough bream to control the spread of weed, and large areas of water were covered up. This prevented the sunlight from penetrating to the bottom, and its benefit was lost to the many bottom-dwelling organisms, resulting in a sterile environment. ■

As part of a courtship display the female crocodile thrusts herself up into the air. She then settles back and watches as the male executes an over-exaggerated and frenzied routine of 'water-bashing'.

Crocodiles pull their prey into the water and kill them by drowning. Prey as large as zebra or buffalo are taken only by really large crocodiles.

Crocodiles ambush prey from the depths of deep murky water. Besides the camouflage offered by the deep water, the croc needs to be able to drown its prey – in this case a young kudu bull. Should the water be shallower than the prey, then a stalemate would result, with the prey escaping the second the reptile released its hold.

ELEPHANTS

Most people remark that a solitary bull must be very lonesome, missing the company of his friends. But he probably knows exactly where his friends are, as they are usually in rumble contact, linking up whenever they are apart with low-frequency sounds, which travel much further than high-frequency sounds. Separated elephants are able to link up at any time with comparative ease, no matter how dense the bush between them.

Elephants roam in cow herds and bull groups. The bulls, who form loose associations, are often seen alone. The cow herds are stable units and comprise anything from one family to many cows and their families. These cows – grandmothers, aunts, sisters, and daughters – are all led by one dominant cow known as the matriarch.

Findings were published in 1986, by Katherine Payne and other researchers, on ele-phants' low-frequency talk. We hear them when they give rumbles from their vocal chords, a noise many people think comes from their stom-achs. They also make noises by fluttering the skin on their foreheads, making sounds below the level of human hearing. These sounds may have many different meanings. Cows in oestrus have a special rumble that is picked up by the bulls, just as the cows pick up the special rum-bles of bulls in musth.

■

JUVENILE DELINQUENT

COMMUNICATION

Early one morning we spotted a cow herd walking briskly down a large elephant path, obviously in transit back to the jesse. One young bull was playing around at the back. He was in high spirits – as elephants often are at this time of day – and was mock-charging the impalas and warthogs close by, just for fun. They would run out of his way, with pained expressions. When he was about 165 yards (150 metres) behind the herd we saw him think 'I'm too far from the family', and suddenly he got back on to the path and followed at a brisk pace.

'A superb time to ambush him', we thought. It is always wonderful to get close to a wild elephant and now a good opportunity presented itself. There was a large combretum bush a yard from the path; if we could quickly sneak up against the bush after the herd had passed we would have a superb view of him. We would also be relatively safe should he spot us. At this age elephants lack confidence and will normally run for the safety of the herd.

He was now about eighty yards (seventy metres) behind the group. As he approached the bush we were hiding behind he had the expression of one who hadn't a care in the world: eyes half-closed; trunk swaying away. As he suddenly spotted us his eyes widened in terror and total disbelief. Then he decided that if he pretended not to have seen us we would not trouble him. His eyes rolled in mock indifference and his pace quickened slightly, but not too much in case his anxiety became obvious. Twenty yards past us he broke into a run and closed with the herd. Now he was all confidence. He attacked a mopane shrub, trumpeting loudly. Then he spun back to face us, letting us know that he was a big, mean bull who would normally not tolerate any nonsense, and had let us off lightly this time. ∎

Elephants' rumbles are part of their language. We saw evidence of this when once driving through a hunting area, where the animals are very wild. We surprised a cow herd of elephants, who were about to cross the road. As we stopped, they turned and fled in the opposite direction. We did not think they would run far, so we decided to track them and have a look. They ran for half a mile (800 metres) then slowed down and stopped in some thicket. When we caught up with them, all were perfectly still, not making a sound. The matriarch must have instructed them all to be silent. They were listening to see if there were any pursuers. We made no sound. Then, as though satisfied, they suddenly started to feed, still moving in the direction in which they had fled. Relaxed elephants normally feed with their eyes half closed, but these had theirs wide open. We soon realized they were only pretending to feed, in case there was a pursuer, assuming that if they did this the pursuer would drop his guard and so make more sound for the elephants to pick up.

Eventually, when absolutely sure that they had not been followed, they suddenly all turned 180 degrees, and resumed their initial direction back to the road. Co-ordinating such varied group activity shows great intelligence and a complex language.

Another time we saw two family groups, feeding about fifty yards apart, all obviously from the same herd. Suddenly one group stopped. So did the other. Then it came across and joined them, and all marched off together. It was time to move on. The matriarch had given marching orders. ∎

Elephants are not territorial, but they roam across a home range, whose size depends on the availability of food and water. At Mana Pools, cow herds on the valley floor roam over about eighty square miles (200 square kilometres). Those whose range includes the escarpment cover an area of about half that.

HABITS OF THE HERD

A cow elephant with her calves. Elephants conceive at around 13 years of age. A cow may be expected to produce eight calves in her lifetime, and the older cows often have three calves of various ages in tow.

Cow herds are conspicuous by their ever-present youngsters. Under normal conditions cows will calve roughly every four years. During poor or drought conditions they will not come into oestrus, and so will not produce calves; their calving intervals will therefore be longer. During optimum conditions the calving interval has been recorded as being as short as 2.7 years. It is thought that the young cows reach puberty later under stressful times, but normally at 11 to 12 years of age – almost the same as humans.

The bull calves reach puberty at around 15 to 16 years of age, and are then expelled from the cow herd; during drought years they are expelled even earlier. They are very boisterous by this stage, and become a nuisance within the group, competing with the youngsters for food when they are quite easily able to survive on their own. Eventually, each time the young bulls start moving into the centre of the herd the adult cows start showing irritability or even aggression towards them. Taking the hint, the bulls continue to follow the group, but remain on the perimeter. Gradually they become more and more daring, and forage further and further away. Eventually they join the bull groups, where they are accepted as the 'new boys' at high school.

The bulls form very loose associations, but, rather like us, they have friends they prefer to be with. You may see a group of five one day, only to find they have split up the next day, some being with other bulls, or alone.

During their wanderings, the elephants often meet up, especially at waterholes, where there are always greetings ceremonies and individuals catching up on the latest gossip. The calves all rush in and play with their friends, whom they may not have seen for a while. Elephants are continually touching and feeling each other, and drape their tunks companionably over their friends or family. When meeting each other one puts its trunk into the other's mouth (in much the same way as we shake hands or kiss to say hello). This behaviour is normally initiated by the subordinate animal. These creatures are intelligent and show behaviour that is very 'human', aiding individuals that are sick or wounded, or helping young animals up steep climbs or descents. After feeding together for a while, the groups move off on their own separate ways.

Through these group meetings, youngsters grow up knowing everyone within the community, and a pecking order is established at a young age. This is important for the young bulls later on in life, when they leave the cow herds, for they know exactly where they stand. As a result, elephants seldom fight seriously, although the bulls spend much time in mock or play fights, testing each others' strengths. ■

SEXUAL CHARACTERISTICS

Adult bulls and cows may be told apart easily by their head shapes. Cows have small heads with pointed foreheads; whereas bulls have big heads with rounded foreheads. The bulls also appear to be more long-legged. Many a time people mistake the sexes when looking at `the obvious', for both cows and bulls have an area of loose skin flapping between their back legs. The bulls have internal testicles and the loose skin between the back legs is the penis sheath. This piece of skin differs from the cows' in that it ends abruptly with an opening for the penis. In the cows, the skin tapers gradually up to the belly.

Internal testicles are common to all members of the elephant family, even the tiny rock rabbits, or dassies. In most animals the testicles are external, as the semen must be kept cooler than body temperature in order to remain fertile. It is not understood how elephants keep their semen fertile when it is at body temperature all the time.

More advanced creatures all seem to have two breasts located between their front legs, and the elephant is no exception.

The time between January and April is the peak time for the elephant bulls to be in musth. This has been likened to a male equivalent of the females coming into season. Both bull and cow African elephants secrete from what is called a temporal gland, and these secretions may mean many different things, depending on their make-up. Certainly many secretions are stress-related. On surprising an elephant we often see a trickle of fresh secretion from the temporal region.

The term `musth' was originally used in reference to Indian elephants, because only Indian bull elephants secreted, and only when in musth. The mahouts (the elephant drivers) knew to tie them up when this happened as they became aggressive. As African elephants all secrete, it was thought they had a different system. The African musth bulls' secretion is of a completely different composition from normal secretion. It is much thicker and flakes white on the sides as it dries. It is also a substantial secretion, the dampness extending to below the jaw.

When in peak musth, African elephants have an almost constant discharge from the penis sheath, causing the tip of the sheath to turn a greenish colour. Many people thought this was some form of sickness. Its colour prompted the

Many people interpret ear-flapping as a sign of aggression in elephants, but actually this motion serves to cool the blood - much like a car radiator. This elephant has a broken ear, perhaps the result of a fight. He has to work twice as hard with his good ear for the same cooling effect, as his broken ear cannot move.

Elephant's ears have a high concentration of veins and arteries. The blood flowing through these is cooled by the flapping motion of the ears.

TEETHING

researcher who exposed the condition, Cynthia Moss, to call it 'green penis syndrome'. This discharge is extremely strong-smelling, and we can often smell that a musth bull has passed before even seeing his spoor with the tell-tale droplets on top.

A musth bull walks around as though challenging the world, head held high. Bulls certainly become more aggressive when in musth, and other bulls seem to respect this.

The musth is an annual event, occurring in each individual at approximately the same time each year. The youngest bull to come into musth, as recorded by Cynthia Moss, was some 27 years old. At this age the condition does not last long, but the older the elephants get the longer the period is each year, and it can eventually last as long as three months. During this time the males actively seek out the females who, it has been shown, are very responsive to them. The females get very excited when they cross the trail of a musth bull. Moss and Poole showed that the females are hassled continuously by the young bulls, but these bulls are kept at a manageable distance if there is a bull in musth present. ∎

Throughout their lives elephants have six sets of upper and lower molars. These sets grow gradually forwards in the mouth as they are pushed from behind by the next generation. Fragments continuously chip off at the front of the mouth until the old molars are completely replaced by new ones. Molars appear at set stages through their lives. In a study carried out in Luangwa National Park in 1979, John Hanks found that the first molar in the mouth is fully formed at 1 year; the second at 2; the third at 6; the fourth at 15; the fifth at 27; and the sixth at 45 years. After the sixth has erupted, the back of the jaw calcifies and no more molars are forthcoming. Rarely, elephants may have a seventh or supernumary molar, which is slightly different in shape. ∎

After measuring and weighing all the organs of a bull killed on an elephant reduction programme, John Hanks found that the penis is about 63 in (160 cm) long and weighs around 112 lb (51 kg). Elephants carry about two pints (one litre) of semen.

When the cusps (ridges) finally wear down on the final set of an elephant's molars, the elephant starts to get thinner and thinner, as it cannot chew its food properly to get maximum digestion. Eventually, at around 60 years of age, it will start to lose condition, and ultimately die. This is an additional means of population control for a beast whose only natural enemy is man, and until a couple of centuries ago even we had only a negligible impact on their populations.

THE ELEPHANT'S HONEYCOMB

Elephants' bones are solid, so they contain no bone marrow, which is where in most other animals red blood cells are manufactured. Instead, they make them in the huge sinus area on the head, called the honeycomb, which also serves to lighten the skull. If the elephant's skull were largely solid bone, like a hippo's, it would have great difficulty keeping its head up all the time. The hippo needs the weight as counterballast, and besides, its head is near ground level most of the time, or supported by water. ■

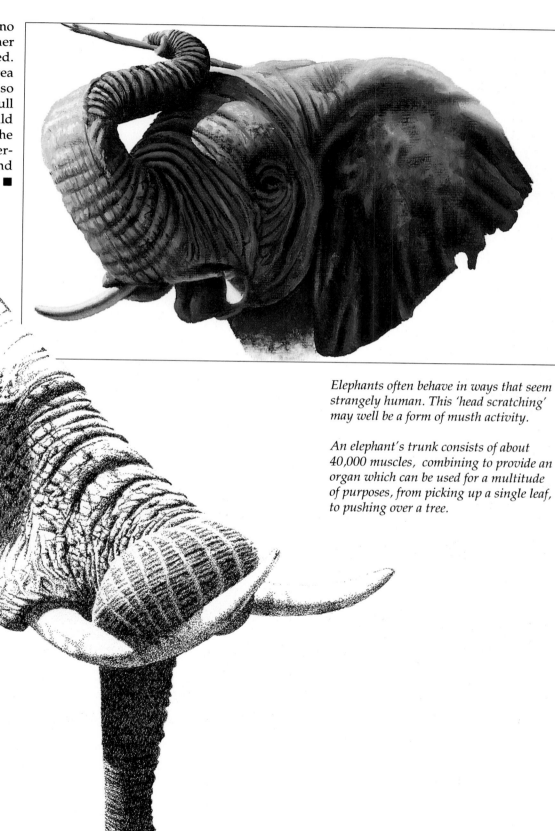

Elephants often behave in ways that seem strangely human. This 'head scratching' may well be a form of musth activity.

An elephant's trunk consists of about 40,000 muscles, combining to provide an organ which can be used for a multitude of purposes, from picking up a single leaf, to pushing over a tree.

A pan in the mopane woodland between showers. In the foreground is a water-filled wallowing place. The elephant has sensed something and is walking off, tail and head raised. The egrets, startled from their pursuit of insects, take to the air with similar wariness. Caught in a shaft of light against the heavy, dark skies, this remarkable scene is a vivid contrast with the usual sombre shades of the bush.

COMMUNITY NESTING

A darter just about to take off, showing its webbed feet.

A goliath heron is an unmistakeable, large bird, which moves with slow ponderous wing-beats. Fish eagles often take advantage of this slowness by attempting to steal prey from them.

By January the heron breeding season is well under way. Herons nest communally, along with cormorants, darters and egrets, in one heronry. The obvious benefit of this arrangement is the multiplicity of eyes and bills to seek out and repel predators. Furthermore, the heronries are usually located on small islands with big trees, making it difficult for even truly persistent predators to get to them. There are soon many young birds of all shapes and sizes, and the air is filled with squawks and croaks from the thriving community.

The egrets are a group of birds within the heron family. The great white egrets prefer to hunt alone in fairly deep water, and `still hunt', that is, wait for the fish to come to them. Then, with their bill poised and neck forward, they strike like lightning. They share the same habitat as the grey herons, and like them, are found in many other places throughout the world. As is usual in nature, however, their diet differs sufficiently for them not to be in direct competition with each other.

Other lone hunters are the little egrets who, by contrast, actively seek out their prey. You will often see them walking in a businesslike way through the shallows, dashing after the small fish they disturb. Sometimes they will stop, moving just one foot around. It is thought that this churning-up motion could attract fish in search of dislodged nourishment. Their legs are black and grey, so camouflaged in the water, but their feet are bright yellow and may look like other fish. Panicked fish nearby may rush to the apparent security of the yellow fish, only to end up in the egret's stomach.

The black egret is a close relative, and although its colour is at the other end of the scale, its feet are exactly the same and must serve the same purpose. However, the black egret offers its prey the added attraction of shade, by fanning out its wings to form an umbrella. With its head under a wing, it waits for fish to be attracted to the shade. If none appears, it quickly jumps up, runs a couple of paces, and umbrellas again. The black egret often benefits from other birds like the yellow-billed storks or spoonbills, by providing this 'safe house' for the unwary fish seeking refuge from their attentions. ∎

COLOUR SIGNALS

SADDLE-BILLED STORKS

Squacco herons sit quietly in the short grass at the edges of the main rivers or the pans. They feed mostly on insects. Living as they do, completely exposed in the open, they are vulnerable to sudden attacks from bigger predatory birds. If there is any potential danger they sit still, looking like a short stump sticking out of the ground. The upper surface and the back of this heron are brown, and the wings fold up to conceal their white colour; this gives the heron a brown appearance, which is good camouflage on the ground. Herons know that falcons need a flying target to attack, so when buzzed by falcons, they remain stationary. If attacked or disturbed by anything else the squacco heron takes to the air, exposing the white wing and tail feathers. The effect is a sudden flash of white, surprising the attacker and allowing the heron to make good its escape.

The painted reed frogs also demonstrate the benefit of colour flashing. If you look closely enough you can often see these frogs near the tops of the reeds. They have beautiful colours of black, white and yellow. Should you disturb them, they will leap away into the reeds. As they leap, they expose the bright-red skin between their legs. This gives the impression of a flash of red, so any predator, such as a heron, will now be looking for something red. On landing, the frog withdraws the red and is now black, white and yellow again.

There are two other small herons who feed on a similar diet to the squacco, so nature places them in slightly different habitats. The green-backed herons hunt from perches on trees fallen into the river, or stumps in the water, always where aquatic vegetation has accumulated in the current. The rufous-bellied herons occupy the pans, remaining on the robust aquatic plants, like the water hyacinth. They do not overlap into the niche occupied by the African jacanas, which, being lighter and with more spreading feet, are able to feed on far less buoyant floating plants. Of the larger herons, the purple heron remains in the dense reed cover of the channels in the Zambezi; and the goliath, the largest heron in the world, hunts in the main river. Its size enables it to occupy far deeper water than any of the other species. ∎

The little egret is unlike other heron types, in that it is very active in pursuit of prey.

A black egret in umbrella pose – creating shade to attract fish and to make it easier to see into the water. The bird then stabs at the fish with its bill.

Another common resident seen at this time is a large bird called the saddle-billed stork. These birds have the same coloration as the painted reed frog, but for no apparent reason. They are unusual in that they hunt like large herons, by wading into shallow water to catch fish and amphibians. However, saddle-billed storks fly with their necks extended, unlike the herons, who keep their necks folded.

Seen either alone, or in pairs, these storks are shy birds. They build their nests in tall trees, making a platform of sticks, which is then lined with reeds, grasses and soil, made deep enough to conceal the birds when sitting on their eggs (both males and females do this) These nests can be as much as a hundred feet (thirty metres) above the ground. Sometimes, when walking under the trees by the river, you come across the carcass of a stork chick, who has inadvertently fallen out of the nest and plummeted down, to be seized upon by some passing predator. ∎

The painted reed frog (also called the bell frog) utilizes a brilliant scare tactic when threatened. Normally, from above, it looks black, yellow and white, but when it leaps up its scarlet underside becomes visible, so the predator looks for this colour as the frog lands. However, upon landing, the frog folds up its legs and becomes black, yellow and white once more.

The egyptian goose is widely distributed
throughout Africa. It seems to nest
anywhere: flattened reeds or grass near the
water, hollow trees, or in the abandoned
nests of other birds.

EGYPTIAN GEESE

The black sparrowhawk is renowned for killing large prey. Its prey here is an egyptian goose.

Many young egyptian geese are on the river in July/August. The older ones form loose flocks, but many still cannot fly and are herded around by the parents. If danger threatens, the youngsters take to the water, and if really pressurized skim across the surface, flapping their wings as they attempt to put as much distance as possible between themselves and the threat. It is strange that more are not taken by crocodiles when they do this.

The adults are very colourful, although their beauty is in contrast to their 'bitchy' attitude to life. They always seem to be having domestic disputes with each other, or anyone unfortunate enough to be nearby. Apart from being slightly bigger, the males are difficult to tell apart from the females, but their calls are different. The males hiss and the females honk. We heard this noise one day, and laughed when we saw one bird laying into another with what looked like a disgruntled housewife's feather duster. The object of this abuse gave a feeble show of defiance, but obviously felt guilty about being out late with the boys again. ∎

Above the wooded areas of the floodplain, where the birds of prey hunt, a peregrine falcon has just raked a laughing dove with its talons. These strikes can often sever the victim's head.

Tawny eagles land on snakes and crush them with their talons. They wait for a short time before beginning to feed.

A fish eagle calling; this beautiful sound can still be heard when the bird is soaring high above its territory.

EAGLES

There has been some dispersal of the resident eagles at this time of year, particularly the bataleurs and tawny eagles. There are, however, big flocks of the migratory steppe eagles. You will see both types feeding on termite alates, but the steppe eagles will be in flocks while the tawny eagles remain single, or form pairs. Wahlberg's eagles are also in evidence now, the thicker woodland being more to their liking for breeding. Come the dry season and they will head north once more, their breeding season over.

The fish eagles are ever-present and continue to be a joy to our ears, with their characteristic call, issued forth with their head thrown back. The male's call is much higher than the female's, and this is particularly noticeable when they call in duet. He is also a little smaller than her – a common feature in birds of prey.

The fish eagles establish territories on a permanent water source. They can afford to breed all year round, but they peak during the dry season. This guarantees a greater hunting success for feeding their young, as in the dry season the water is clearer and they are thus more easily able to spot their prey.

Each breeding pair defends a territory of about half a mile (one kilometre) of river front. As well as calling, they display visually to advertise their ownership. This they do by perching high up on tall trees, where their white heads and breasts are highly visible. The immature eagles, like the young of many birds, look scruffy and unkempt. The young fish eagles take about five years to reach maturity. When they are able to fend for themselves, or when the next brood is on the way, they are chased out of the territory. They then have to eke out an existence in the marginal areas, and are often seen foraging around pans. These young birds, with their dark eye stripe, are often mistaken for ospreys.

The ospreys seem to be increasing now, and have been seen occasionally on the lower river. Their feeding habits are different from those of the fish eagle, who stoops from a perch. They hunt from the air and plunge right down, often below the water's surface. When they re-emerge they fly about six feet (two metres) above the water, and shake the water off their feathers before continuing on their way. ∎

The fish eagle grasps its prey with one foot to enable it to perch easily upon landing.

THE DDT CONTROVERSY

Recent studies have shown that predatory birds at the top of the food chain are now faced with a new threat to their existence. This threat comes as a direct result of the vast quantities of DDT which have been used in a government programme to rid areas of the tsetse fly. The tsetse fly is locally regarded as a stumbling block to rural development. It can cause a disease known as Nagana in animals, and Trypanosomiasis (sleeping sickness) in human beings. In both cases the disease is severely debilitating and can result in death. Trypanosomiasis, however, has been responsible for fewer than half a dozen reported human fatalities in the twenty-five years prior to 1992 – a fraction of the total figure of disease-related deaths during the same period. The main reason for the onslaught against the tsetse fly is because of its effect on domestic livestock, and millions of dollars have been spent on an exercise to pour tons of insecticide into our finely balanced environment.

In other parts of the world, environmentally damaging pesticides, DDT being one of them, have been banned. It has been proved that these pesticides eventually end up in both human and wild species' systems via the food chain. DDT has even been discovered in human breast-milk samples taken in Harare in 1988.

Supporters of the DDT campaign claim that the insecticide is sprayed only on the tsetse fly's preferred resting sites, which are small areas not near water. Thus, they maintain, water contamination is kept to a bare minimum, with absolutely no danger to humans. With such vast quantities being dumped around, however, it was inevitable that a percentage of DDT would enter the food chain via the water system. The paranoia about the tsetse fly has led to bush and woodland being bulldozed, millions of wild animals being slaughtered (some 'boffin' had the idea that if you get rid of the carriers then you get rid of the fly!) and now, finally, the noble and beautiful eagles look like becoming another casualty. Many of these birds rely to a great extent on fish for their protein intake.

Examination of dead fish eagles has revealed lethal levels of inorganic mercury in their livers. The mercury was traced back to mines operating in the area. DDT accumulates within body tissues in much the same way, and DDT in the water system will inevitably be taken up by the fish, and then by the eagles. The disastrous effects of DDT on the ecosystem are of much greater concern than even those of mercury, as some researchers anticipate a population crash among the top of the food chain species. Recent findings have revealed widespread contamination in fish eagle eggs, along with subsequent eggshell thinning. The tiger fish, which constitute an important food source for the fish eagle, has lately shown an increased contamination level sixty times greater than previously recorded. ■

A fish eagle robbing an osprey.

A bataleur eagle in flight.

VULTURES

Midday is definitely the time to take it easy. Lions are seldom seen moving around at this time, preferring to lie up in the shade.

With the coming of the rains most animals have dispersed into the valley interior. Although the herbivores find this a time of plenty, the vultures have a harder time to find food: these birds now have a larger area to cover, over thicker bush, with fewer kills taking place beneath them. They must rely on the fat reserves accumulated during the previous months to see them through this period. Many of the weaker vultures will fall by the wayside to become, in turn, food for other scavengers.

American Westerns have led people to believe that when vultures circle in a group, there is a kill beneath. This is not so: they are suspended in a thermal, circling to gain height. When you see vultures appearing from nowhere, plummeting from the sky, undercarriage lowered as they approach, then one can be reasonably sure there is a kill beneath. (However, they also do this in the midday heat when they come down to drink.) When one observes this plummeting action it can sometimes prove rewarding to make your way to the point of descent. Once it is established that there is a kill, great care must be taken when approaching it. You will know that the predators are still feeding if the vultures are perched up in the trees.

One day, at a kill, we watched vultures feeding off a hippo carcass. Nearby we also saw a young male lion resting in the shade of a dead mahogany tree. He watched us with a sleepy wariness; the warm temperature and his full stomach meant it was definitely siesta time. Cautiously we approached the carcass. The vultures, now obesely full, struggled into the air. Some needed a few leaps and bounds before achieving this, but all were soon perched on trees nearby. (At times like these they must wish they were wild dogs, who could hold their ground even at the approach of these interfering humans.) Now all that remained was the lifeless form in an arena surrounded by watching eyes. Then, to our astonishment, we noticed movement from inside the rib-cage – a closer inspection revealed a white-backed vulture, well-entangled in some strands of hippo hide. Though it struggled feebly it seemed to have accepted its fate, and even after we cut away the sinew it still did not believe it was free. Eventually, after much prodding, the vulture suddenly got the message and burst out – rather

Vultures have different functions at kills. Some put their heads and bodies right into the carcass. Most vultures' diet consists of carrion, and especially offal.

The hooded vulture tends to hang around on the periphery of kills, ducking in occasionally for the odd scrap of food.

A white-backed vulture's head gets right inside the carcass of its prey.

like an athlete leaving the starting blocks. To our utter surprise it charged straight at us! We parted and let the kamikaze hero pass between us. You could imagine the vulture's relief at then seeing, instead of a set of pearly gates, close thicket in which to disappear. As it hopped away it was clear to us that the struggle in the carcass had drained it of so much energy that flight had become impossible.

When vultures fly, they gain sufficient height in the thermals, then disperse, each to its own airspace. From there they mount their never-ending search for carrion. Should a bird locate a kill, it will immediately start to drop out of the sky, to get there as quickly as possible. This will not go unnoticed by the bird next door, who will immediately follow, and so on, with bird following bird. This is how so many vultures are able to arrive at a kill in such a short time.

The four types of vulture at Mana Pools avoid direct competition by different bill sizes and/or feeding habits (Mundy, 1982). The largest one, the powerful lappet-faced vulture, usually arrives last, to prize off large chunks of meat and any remaining skin. The white-headed vulture feeds on smaller pieces, like intestines and shreds off bones. The little hooded vulture waits on the outskirts and feeds on all the scraps and sinews. These three vultures are all feathered up to their heads, which are bald: blood from their feeds would stick their feathers together in a place it is hard for them to reach while cleaning.

The fourth type, the white-backed vulture, avoids the other species by feeding from inside the carcass, either by putting its head beneath the ribs to get to the inside, or, when possible, by climbing right in. Due to this feeding behaviour, their necks would also become clotted up, so they are unfeathered, having just fine soft down there. They can reach the remainder of their bodies while preening. ∎

VULTURES ON THE IVORY TRAIL

A crocodile's nest that has been uncovered by a leguaan might be noticed by a vulture – forever the opportunist.

Marabou storks are often found at carcasses taking on the role of a vulture. They are, however, opportunists, and also eat rodents and insects.

Currently in Africa we are experiencing a vast amount of game slaughter for profit. Some killing is done legally, and for the correct reasons, but most is done by poachers, some of whom are armed with the latest automatic weapons. It is this deadly firepower that has resulted in the near-extinction of the black rhino and the deaths of many thousands of elephants.

When we see vultures dropping from the sky, we pray that we are seeing an act of nature, not stepping on the bloody ivory trail passing through Africa. It is almost a pleasure to find an elephant that has died of natural causes. Like a knight laid to rest with his sword, the sight of an elephant with tusks intact has a nobility about it. Heathcote Williams wrote in *Sacred Elephant* 'The elephant is shat upon with greater honesty by vultures.' How true.

Vultures descend on an elephant carcass in great numbers; branches creak under the strain as they wait for the predators to have their fill. It is nature's way that the death of one animal should provide nourishment for thousands of others – from the vulture to the maggot. ∎

*Birds of prey choose dead trees with good
visibility for their perches, as well as to
overnight on. Towards sunset vultures
and eagles settle, as the air is cooling and
there are no thermals to lift them.*

APRIL

This lilac-breasted roller is attacking a moth, which is shaped and coloured like a wasp (this is an anti-predator device).

vivid colours are in strong contrast to the drab bush hues of its surroundings.

We wonder at the incredible navigation skills of the many migrants that enable them to travel thousands of miles to destinations some have never seen. For some it will be their first time ever, and they will fly the route on what must be pure instinct. How many will perish on the way – not only as a result of adverse weather conditions, or from sheer exhaustion, but as victims of the many hunters' guns fired into the flocks for fun, as a mere leisure pursuit?

AN ELEPHANT COOLS OFF

An elephant bull stirs in the shadows. It is the hottest time of day, and the humidity has spurred his thirst. He ambles slowly down to the waterhole and, clearing the surface with his trunk, he briefly draws some water and squirts it behind him, on to the soil. The surface cleared to his satisfaction, he draws in a trunkful of water and inserts his trunk in his mouth. We can hear the water gush down into that cavernous throat.

Eight trunkfuls later – about sixteen-gallons (sixty-litres) worth, he remains motionless for a minute or two, as though pondering his next move, then lumbers to a muddy patch on the other side of the pan. Skilfully collecting mud up on the end of his trunk, he aims it with accuracy to the various hot parts of his body – under his legs, behind his ears, on his back and his sides. Besides cooling him, the mud must also give him some respite from biting insects, as well as the sun on his back.

He starts to move off, pausing briefly by some fine soil. Following the same process as with the mud, he covers himself with dust. His talcum-powdering complete, he moves off once more with the same purposeful gait, and vanishes into the thicket nearby. We marvel at having been so close to this massive beast, a gentleman of the wilderness, and he entirely oblivious to our presence.

BACK AT THE CAMP

Back in camp, we sneak off for a siesta after lunch. Our room is a hive of activity. There are many mud-wasp nests, and the wasps are coming in and out, either with mud from the edges of pans, or with newly captured jumping spiders they have recently paralysed with their stings. These are pushed into the mud capsules,

I t is April in the Zambezi valley and, as the rainy season is just starting to tail off, the atmosphere is hot, humid and oppressive. There is little shade around. Even the albidas offer little respite, having been leafless for the last three months. Except for during the early morning and late afternoon there is little movement from the animals in daylight hours. Feeding takes place mainly during the cool of evening. Food is abundant and the herbivores are sleek and well fed. They can afford to spend less time in search of food.

The birds are quiet now, save for the occasional call, their breeding season complete. For many it is time to prepare for the long northbound migration, which will take many as far afield as France or the CIS. Others will travel only as far as equatorial Africa, but most will remain, or just move locally. One remaining resident is the beautiful lilac-breasted roller, whose which are sealed once the wasp has laid her egg within. When the larva hatches, it will feed on the paralysed jumping spiders.

Next, in comes a brilliant emerald-coloured wasp, called a cuckoo wasp. She is a parasite of the mud wasp and, after a short search, she locates one of the many mud-wasp nests in the room. Quickly entering, she lays her egg inside one. When it hatches her larva will feed on the host larva and its food supply.

In the afternoon we venture out again. There are many migrant European rollers in evidence who, though they are pretty in their shades of blue, are no match for our lilac-breasted rollers. There are also many other migrants to be seen before they set off – sand martins, European swifts, and swallows.

DANGER IN THE PANS

We stop at a big pan and three large crocodiles slither into the water. Many move from the river into these pans at this time of year, to take advantage of the easier hunting conditions. No large pans are safe, and you should exercise caution before wading across the smaller ones.

Often we come across a pan completely covered in water hyacinth, and occasionally there might be crocodiles feeding on a carcass in one of these pans. Like children playing under a blanket, the hyacinth rolls and rocks as the crocodiles fight for food beneath it. A tell-tale leg might suddenly break the surface as the carcass is rolled over by the reptiles. When these pans dry up, the crocodiles walk back to the Zambezi.

Also found in water hyacinth are hippo. A comical sight is a hippo's head covered in hyacinth peeping out at us – like an aunt wearing a terrible hat at a wedding. The hippo is probably a young bull who was unable to withstand the aggression of territorial bulls and so moved to the security of the pans.

INSIDE THE JESSE BUSH

It is at this time of year that elephant and rhino paths have become tunnels in the jesse, so thick is the bush. Extreme alertness is of paramount importance, as you will literally bump into these huge animals before you see them. Should you need to disappear at speed, you will often be able to go only backwards or forwards, for the bush on either side of the path is virtually impenetrable, and there may well be no substantial tree to climb.

The heat of the April afternoons can prove too much for the elephant calves. It is an ideal time to have a quick snooze.

Venturing into the jesse can be rewarding, though. Many shy and rarely seen creatures, like the nyala, live here. Nyala are close relatives of the kudu. The males are very handsome, with their shaggy chocolate-brown coats, a total contrast with the red-brown females. The females are a lot smaller than the males, and look very like bushbuck, which belong to the same family and sometimes share the same habitat.

You might occasionally glimpse a Sharpe's grysbuck scuttling away from you. They are so small they look rather like large hares. The crested guinea fowl are a funny sight, the thatch-like bunch of feathers on the tops of their heads make them look like an avian equivalent of rastafarians. Narina trogons are found here too. They are beautiful birds with vivid red-and-green plumage. They are seldom seen, but their harsh booming call during the summer months gives them away. ∎

BUSHPIGS

Bushpigs are residents of the edges of thicket, emerging after dark to feed out in the open. Unlike the warthogs, they can afford to feed when most predators are active, as they forage in groups for protection, and in addition, are more aggressive.

They are well-designed for living in thick undergrowth, being streamlined, so they can fly like bullets through thick bush. On the other hand, their cousins, the warthogs, are designed for their plains existence: big fronts and sagging backs. Warthogs move easily in and out of holes, the stocky front and big head ideal for blocking their burrow entrances.

A similar comparison may be made with impala and bushbuck. Bushbuck and bushpig, both dense-bush dwellers, have arched backs which taper down towards the front. This is an ideal design for their environment. The impala, however, has a higher shoulder, and its body is better suited for sprinting and leaping. ∎

By remaining motionless bushbuck can remain undetected in the bush.

RHINO COUNTRY

The Zambezi valley has until recently housed the world's biggest concentration of black rhinoceros, but the poaching onslaught of the past three years has reduced their numbers drastically, and now only a few remain. The poachers are mostly active during the summer months, when the bush is at its thickest. You would need to be within half a mile (one kilometre) of them to hear their shots, and even then it is difficult to know from exactly which direction they came. Locating poachers from the air is almost impossible. What makes the problem even more frustrating is that the area is adjacent to the Zambian border, and an international boundary always complicates things. With little co-operation from Zambia, the skeleton anti-poaching staff in Zimbabwe is unable to take much effective action.

It is a sad fact that the black rhino, which has been with us for thousands of years, is now faced with extinction. The few surviving black rhino in the Zambezi valley find the jesse ideal for their browsing needs. Their cousins, the white rhino prefer the good grazing to be found on the open plains of Zimbabwe.

The two rhino species differ in many ways. One difference is size – the white rhino species is the larger animal; also, the white rhino is a grazer, and the black rhino is predominantly a browser. The white rhino has a square lip for grazing, and this led to it being called the wide-mouthed rhino by the early Afrikaans settlers. A misinterpretation of terms ensued, and it became known as the white rhino, although both species are the same colour. A final identification is that when a rhino and calf trot away, the black rhino leads its calf, and the white rhino will push its calf ahead of it. This could probably be explained by their selected habitats. It is more difficult to run through thick bush, and if a calf led the way it would soon be a shambles. On the open plains chased animals are attacked from the rear because they are weak or slow. A white rhino mother can therefore better defend her calf by covering the vulnerable rear.

Black rhinos are far more aggressive than the white, and are fairly unpredictable. They may be persuaded to come right up to you if you mimic their squeal-like call, although it is a good plan to be out of their reach when doing so. We recall with amusement the faces of seven of our guests, jam-packed atop a large termite

The black rhino helps to make paths through the bush. The bush can grow over the paths to form a tunnel effect.

mound, with an irate rhino snorting at the base. The whites of their eyes were distinctly visible from fifty yards away!

Rhinos are territorial and mark out their territories by forming middens (dunghills) at various points around their area. At these middens, you will see where they have scraped the dung with their feet to spread it over a wider area. It is also thought that dung caught up between their hooves during this action helps spread their scent further as they walk away.

People often confuse hippo tracks with those of rhinos. The four small toes of the hippos near the front of the foot are sometimes indistinct, and may resemble the large central toe of the black rhino's three-toed foot. The two tracks can be distinguished by the toes on the sides of the feet: hippos' point outward, much like our thumbs, and rhinos' run parallel to the spoor. ■

The attentions of this amorous rhino were unwanted, so the female ran under a branch to knock him off.

DUNG BEATLES

A dung beetle rolling a ball of dung to be used for feeding or breeding.

The dung beetles, or scarabs, are famous in ancient Egyptian mythology for their part in rolling the sun around the earth. They are also exceptionally important because of the part they play in breaking down dung and making it available in nutrient form for the uptake of plants again. Most species bury the dung in one way or another, and in so doing also trap nitrogen in the soil, which would otherwise be lost into the atmosphere. They also help control the fly population by making less dung available for flies to breed in. This is the reason why dung beetles were imported into Australia.

Dung beetles may be divided into three groups. The endocoprids, paracoprids, and the telecoprids. It is easy to remember the difference between them if you remember that on arrival at the dung, the **end**ocoprids have reached the **end**

of their journey, and they breed and feed inside the dung. Because of this they are the smaller of the three. The **para**coprids make tunnels directed beneath the dung – like a **para**chute descent – and they take the dung down these tunnels to feed and breed. The **tele**coprids, like **tele**phones, are long-distance operators. They pat the dung into a ball with their front legs, which are modified rakes. Then they roll their dung a distance away from the heap and bury it for their breeding and feeding. This habit of burying the dung also means that they avoid competition with other insects, and can eat their meal at leisure.

These scarabs will always have mites, normally in the region where the head joins the body. There seems to be some form of symbiotic relationship between the two, and it is thought that if you remove the mites the dung beetles will die. You may also find minute flies on them, which seem reluctant to leave. It seems as though these flies, which must also feed and breed in the dung, are probably not as adept at locating it, and so catch a free ride to the dung on the dung-locating experts. They may, in return, keep the dung beetle clean of the dung that must accumulate on its body.

When breeding, only the male rolls the dung ball, the female remaining firmly attached as it is being rolled, without offering any assistance. Although she remains to one side, in order to keep out of the way as much as possible, she frequently ends up underneath. This does not seem to bother her.

As in human society, there are always citizens with poor ethics who wait in ambush and try to take over the ball for themselves, rather than roll their own. This brings to mind the image of a looter with a large television set, kicking out at fellow looters because he is powerless to use his over-burdened arms. The dung beetle uses his rakes like this in an attempt to repel attackers before making good his escape with the ball.

Once the male and female are established in their underground home and they have collected about five balls, they mate and she lays an egg inside each ball. When the young hatch they feed on the dung for one to two months before maturing into beetles. During this stage, though, the young dung beetles can be predated upon by the honey badgers. If the nests are discovered, the honey badgers dig down, and eat the larvae with relish. ∎

African hunting dogs running along sands recently deposited by the Zambezi. They are not pursuing prey - if they were their heads would be down and their ears back - these dogs are lolloping and frisking their way back from drinking on the river's edge.

WILD DOGS GO HUNTING

Wild dogs – or, more correctly, African hunting dogs – are not territorial animals. They are nomadic, roaming over vast distances when not breeding, generally killing animals the size of impala, or sub-adults of larger species. It is not uncommon, however, for them to tackle adult zebra and wildebeest.

Unfortunately, cattle also appear on their menu, and this has led to their heavy persecution by man. Beyond the borders of our national parks they have been virtually eradicated.

They differ from other members of the Canidae family in having only four toes on the front foot. When hunting, they rely to a large extent on sight, and not so much on hearing. Rather, they use their large ears for long-distance communication between different members of the pack. They have a complex social structure, and lavish greeting ceremonies take place each time the pack is about to hunt. In fact, their whole social behaviour is very similar to that other respected carnivore's, the wolf. This similarity, as well as their pretty coloration, has given them their scientific name, *Lycaon pictus,* meaning 'painted wolf'.

Wild dogs are the only predators that allow their young to feed before the adults on a kill. The adults will, if the pups are too young to follow, regurgitate meat for them and for any other adult remaining behind when they return to the den. They hunt early in the morning and late in the afternoon as a rule, but like all predators, will hunt at any time if they are hungry. Just prior to hunting the dogs get very excited and utter yelping, whining sounds, accompanied by much licking and greeting.

One day we were fortunate enough to come across a pack of seven wild dogs lying beside a pan, resting in the midday heat. We settled down to study and photograph them in anticipation of an eventful afternoon. The dogs, of course, had noticed us. One dog, with his head resting on another's back, actually moved his ears when we made a noise. Other than that the animals hardly moved for what seemed like hours. We began coughing and fake sneezing in an effort to motivate them. We stretched, yawning loudly, and even stood up suddenly, walking around a little before sitting down again. Nothing moved. About two hours later we were watching them in silence, having by now exhausted all topics of conversation. Suddenly all the dogs bombshelled. They ran off in all directions, and stopped about forty yards (thirty-five metres) away. Just as quickly, they all turned and trotted back to the water. One lay in the mud, soiling the beautiful white tip on his tail. It was so sudden that by the time we spoke they had all lain down again. We had not heard anything – there was no audible signal given.

As the temperature dropped, so we noticed the wild dogs getting restless. Then, by now late afternoon, the pack was up and moving off. Soon they were trotting along the fringe of the

A wild dog killing an impala ewe. These efficient killers have been seriously reduced in numbers by humans, who dislike them for their way of killing.

mopane. Two peeled off from the rest of the pack and went sniffing around in the vicinity of a herd of impalas, while the rest of the pack trotted disinterestedly on.

Suddenly, like bullets, the two exploded towards the impala herd, which scattered. The dogs had already singled out an individual, and followed her towards some thicket. We decided that they would never catch her, as she was too far ahead. They all disappeared into the thicket, and after what must have been about twenty seconds, they all reappeared, the two dogs now right on her tail. (What happens is that the prey never runs in a straight line, but always tries to corner back to the rest of its group, or just stay within its home range. The dog or dogs at the back of the chase simply cut the corner each time, and in so doing lessen the distance between the prey and themselves, giving themselves a better chance of success.)

The impala ran towards us, making a low moaning sound, as if realizing she was doomed, and the dogs pulled her down less than a hundred feet (thirty metres) from our vehicle. From the moment she went down she made almost no effort to struggle. She had given up the fight

and the dogs almost casually disembowelled her. Impala ewes have no horns; their only defence is their speed. She was dead in just over a minute. Although it looked so terrible a fate, she seemed in deep shock and probably felt little or no pain.

No more than a mere fifteen minutes after the impala kill, in the last of the daylight all that remained were her head and ribcage, the rest having been bolted down or carried away by these seven animals.

We returned to camp, amazed at the spectacle we had just witnessed. Early the next morning we returned to the spot to have a quick look. Hyenas had been there after the wild dogs, and had run off with head and ribcage. All that remained were some stomach contents, a red bloodstain, and a couple of droppings. It struck us how efficient nature is – and how unimportant we are in the system. The impala we watched yesterday, running towards us, giving that bleating moan, was now part of the wild dog and hyena droppings. After a couple of rains, that same impala would be part of a new blade of grass growing up through the soil to be eaten by, perhaps, another impala. ∎

The minimum number of wild dogs needed to make a viable pack is five or six. When most of the wild dogs are out hunting, one or two will remain behind to look after the young. The 'nannies' and puppies are fed by regurgitation.

A male leopard enjoying the last of the sun in the grass on the edge of the floodplain. The air is clear and the light clean, the dust-haze dispelled by a rainstorm. Leopards may be found in all habitats, but probably spend least time in the jesse, which is not the best hunting environment during the lean time of year.

Buffalo sometimes retreat during the midday heat into the thick grass of the vetiveria for security and shade. The red-billed oxpecker, seen here on the buffalo, lives off various ungulates by picking ticks off their bodies. Ticks are found mostly in the ears, nostrils and under the tail of their host. The oxpeckers also eat the scabs and drink the blood from flesh wounds.

Vetiveria is ideal cover for lions. The grass can be so thick that predators can approach to within a few feet of their unsuspecting prey. Buffalo have to rely on their acute sense of smell, and even the behaviour of the red-billed oxpecker (their early-warning system) to avoid becoming a prey statistic.

THE COOL DRY SEASON

The cool dry season extends from May to August. This is Zimbabwe's autumn and winter. There may be some drizzle, but any rain is unusual, and the skies are normally clear and blue. The temperature may drop as low as 45°F (8°C) for short periods during the night, rising quickly after sunrise to a high of about 77°F (25°C). In extreme conditions temperatures can drop to around 41°F (5°C).

The first drop in temperature is felt in May, a sure indication that winter is on its way. The rainy season has ended and the bush has started to dry out. Most of the migrants have begun their long annual journeys, although the wood and common sandpipers are still with us. They are among the last to leave, but the first to return in spring. Other birds, like the black coucal, are the last to arrive and the first to leave.

The greenshanks leave behind their first-year birds to overwinter. The following year these now sexually mature birds will make their first long migration, which takes them across to eastern Europe with perfect navigation.

VETIVERIA

The vetiveria is tall grass that grows in dense stands on many places on the floodplain. It grows to about nine feet (three metres) in summer, and is home to a great many animals all year round, including many dangerous species – lion, buffalo, hippo, and elephant.

At times the grass is so tall you can only just see the elephants' backs above it, with their attendant cattle egrets perched on top – unable, in this dense environment, to run along the ground to pick up the insects disturbed by the elephants' feet. Similarly, an egret can sometimes be seen perched above the reeds. Knowing their habits, this appears as a very strange sight, until one gets closer and sees that the bird is actually perched on a buffalo resting at the water's edge.

Vetiveria has a lurking wildlife population within it, which gives it the name 'adrenalin grass'. It is wise, when on foot, to treat these grassy areas with respect, and to avoid them if possible. Many a time we have been walking close by when we have heard the unmistakable low warning growl of lions, or a buffalo has suddenly stood up and poked its head out of the grass. For this reason we always make enough noise for any nearby animal to hear us coming. To surprise them suddenly could spoil your whole day. ■

RUTTING SEASON

Impalas, stimulated by the drop in temperature, have started their rutting season, building up to a peak around the full moon. It is strange how the lunar cycle seems to have an effect on many things. (This lunar timing might occur because hunting is less successful in bright light, so the predators decrease their hunting activities until conditions are more favourable.) Rutting is the establishing of dominance among the males, and the setting-up of territories by the dominant rams. This entails many mock fights, and occasional real ones, which often result in other males joining in, with the whole lot running around in circles, tails erect. Their tails flare out, and the white hairs stand on end in a display of aggression. Many a time people mistake the noise the rams make for those of lions, not believing that these delicate little animals could make such a sound.

The areas of best grazing are taken up by the dominant males to establish their territories. This they do by scent-marking the occasional shrub within the territory by means of their occipital gland, which is located on the forehead. This is why they are often seen rubbing their foreheads on the bushes, as though scratching. They also return to defecate, like rhinos, on their middens, which the females use too; this further helps to mark their territory.

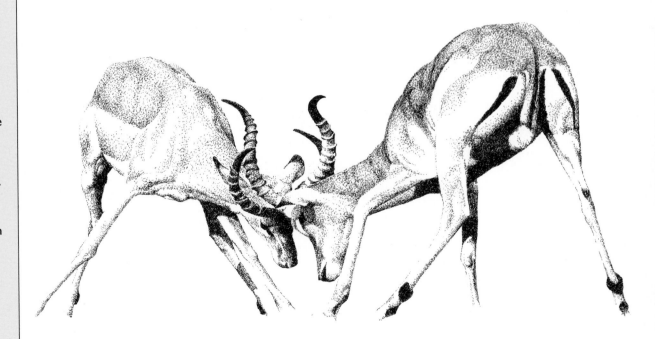

Impala rams fighting during the rutting season when, in order to breed, they have to establish their dominance over other males.

*A cattle egret gets an eagle's-eye view of
the vetiveria - the tall grasslands – from
atop an elephant's back.*

Two serval kittens play in the early morning on the edge of the vetiveria - an area of tall, rank grass. Their coats blend perfectly into the yellow-and-black coloration of the grasses. The hollow tree next to the cats provides a refuge for them in case of danger.

When rutting, the impala rams drop their guard and predators are quick to take advantage. A large part of the leopard's diet consists of impala. This leopard's aggressive posture is possibly the result of the close proximity of another male leopard, or any other impending threat, such as hyenas challenging for a kill.

Finally, if no females are within their boundaries, the impala rams spend a lot of time standing centrally within their territory area, prominently displaying themselves visually.

As the female herds move through each dominant male's territory, they are herded by each ram, who is trying to keep them in his area for as long as possible. This period is also the time when the females come into season, so the longer each male has them in his territory, the more chances he will have to mate, and thus spread his genes. The tactics employed in doing this are often really amusing. Each time the females start feeding towards one of his boundaries, the male will stand between them and the boundary, acting as a block. Sometimes he has to herd them back aggressively, and when all else fails, he may even pretend to see something dangerous in the neighbouring territory, by staring intently there and alarm-snorting. However, when the females are tired of his tactics, they will eventually make a break for it into the welcoming attentions of the next male.

This process is nature's way of ensuring that no weak male ever has the chance to breed. Only the dominant males hold territories, and holding a territory is the only way of securing

breeding rights. So, although only the best genes are being spread, with the females going from one territory to the next a good variation of the best breeding stock is achieved. The territorial rams will not tolerate any males of a year old or more within their territories, and are continuously having to discipline them. The young rams form herds known as bachelor herds, which contain much good up-and-coming breeding stock. In these herds they are relaxed, and able to develop in strength and confidence.

When one of the younger rams feels he is in a position to challenge one of the territorial rams, he will do so. Although many rams hold a territory for some years, others are quickly defeated in these fights, and the ousted rams join the bachelor herds. There is a lot of pressure involved in holding a territory. You must mate with the females, herd them constantly, chase out males all the time, be involved in the odd fight, and stand, head held high, to advertise yourself. This leaves little time for eating, and these males certainly lose a lot of condition.

The rutting season over, all returns to normal, but the dominant males still remain in their territories. They just become more tolerant and maybe range over a wider area. ∎

MAINTAINING THE MALE / FEMALE RATIO

In nature it is the females who must be protected, for they are the baby producers, and the more females there are to produce young, the more viable is the population. Males – and this hurts – are expendable in the system, as a small number of males can fertilize many females. For this reason you will find that in wild populations the sex ratio of males to females will be around 1:4, yet the young are born in a 1:1 sex ratio. The ratio changes as each generation grows up because the males are less alert, being so tied up in who is more dominant than who, or in losing face to the other. This results in more males falling prey to the ever-watchful predators. Also, young inexperienced females are never thrown out of the herds as predator bait, as happens to the males.

Some research was once done on two herds of impala. The male to female ratio of one group was 12:1; and the other 1:12. The groups were fairly large. In both cases conception was poor, and it is thought that when there are too many males, so much time is spent rutting that little is left for mating. In the other group, the absence of rutting may have meant no stimulus to bring the females on heat.

Whatever the reason for such a disparity, it must play a part in the control of populations during and immediately after droughts. During a drought, more females die than males, due to the extra burden of their young. This now creates an excessive number of males, meaning that fewer females are available to conceive the following season. This keeps the population low until the vegetation has recovered.

One year, after a drought at Mana Pools, and in conditions of excellent visibility, a group of us counted all the impala males and females over a twenty-mile (thirty-kilometre) stretch, and the sex ratio was 2.7:1. ■

This impala ram is in prime condition, and holds his head high to advertise his territory to all around.

TERMITE ARCHITECTURE

A dove on a termite mound. It is thought that the formic acid produced by ants helps to kill parasites in birds' feathers.

(right) *Matabele ants, about one inch (2.5 cm) long, are giants to the termites they prey on.*

Termite soldier (left) *and worker* (right)

Microhodotermes are small termites that nest underground in many different types of habitat. They do not build high mounds to live in, like the macrotermes termites. Now that the dung beetles have gone into hibernation, it is these termites who take over the important task of breaking down dung. They quickly move on to freshly dropped dung and cover it with an outer layer of mud, as they do with any food. They then feed on the dung from inside this clay shelter, which protects them from their predators outside.

Much more famous are the macrotermes, who are responsible for those huge mounds, often ten feet (three metres) high, and so characteristic a feature of the African savannah. If one should open up a mound, a couple of minutes will pass before you begin to see the first of the soldier termites (who have probably become aware of the hole because of the temperature drop inside the mound). These termites have come out to defend the mound against any intruders. Following them, when the coast is clear, come the workers who, with the least possible delay, close up the opening. Undefended holes in the termitarium leave the termites vulnerable to attack by predators, such as the dreaded matabele ants.

Matabele ants are large and black, with powerful jaws and a sting to match. They arrive in large columns to attack the termites. The scouts reconnoitre the area first and if it seems worthwhile to attack, return home to summon the troops, leaving a pheromone trail to be followed on returning. After a sucessful raid the ants can be seen marching back again in their column, their jaws packed with termites.

Deeper down in the opened mound you will discover some larg chambers containing strange objects: the 'fungus gardens'. Chewed food is brought from the surface into the mound and compacted. Fungus acts on the compacted food, forming these weird gardens in the process.

Termites are unable to digest the cellulose in the wood they eat as they lack the necessary bacteria in their digestive system, so the fungus, made up of naturally occurring protozoa and bacteria in the area, does the job for them. The termite then eat the fungus. Workers can also feed fellow workers by passing on partially digested food, by excretion or by regurgitation. ∎

101 USES FOR A TERMITE MOUND

The termite mound forms an ideal rubbing post for both warthogs and elephants. Abandoned mounds also make good homes for a variety of creatures. Dwarf and banded mongooses often live in them, along with snakes. Porcupines prefer to live in the larger holes dug by the foraging antbears into the base of the termitarium.

Monitor lizards have been recorded breaking open termitaria and laying their eggs inside. The constant humid warmth of the termitarium is perfect for the eggs to incubate. The termites will not harm them, so they are safe inside. Shortly after the lizard has completed its clutch of eggs, the termites replaster the hole it made. When the young hatch, they dig their way out and off they go.

Antbears create numerous holes while digging in search of termites, and these are modified by warthogs into homes. Warthogs cannot dig holes, and would be susceptible to predation without the aid of these antbears. Antbears never destroy the mounds. If their initial digs are successful, the termites quickly move downward, eventually making the antbear's efforts unproductive, and he moves on to the next mound within his territory.

The soldiers of the trinervitermes, or snouted termites, use chemical warfare, by squirting predators with secretions from glands in their heads. Therefore, a predator can only eat at that mound for as long as it takes the soldiers to arrive on the scene. Then, once again, he must depart for the next mound.

One possible use of termite mounds relates to our occasional observations of birds lying on open ground with their wings spread. This is called `anting' by some people, because it is believed that when the birds do this, they disturb ants, deflecting them from their paths, so that they run all over them. While doing this the ants release a chemical, formic acid, which helps rid the birds of parasites. We have seen a laughing dove on a termite mound, and wonder whether she was there for a similar reason. ∎

Elephants use termite mounds as convenient scratching posts.

Some termites cover their food with a layer of mud, to protect themselves from light so they can forage during the day.

*A baboon on sentry duty on a termite
mound in the floodplain. Sentries, posted
all round the troop's perimeter, are so
vigilant that it is almost impossible to
approach them unseen.*

BABOON TROOPS

Baboons also use these termite mounds, but for an entirely different reason. The mounds act as good lookout posts in all areas, but especially where predators are plentiful. Sentries are posted all around the perimeter of the troop, and are most often up trees. So good is their lookout system that it is almost impossible to approach a troop of baboons unseen.

This system cannot be maintained without strong discipline, which is carried out by the big males. Anyone stepping out of line receives a good hiding. It just takes a hard stare by one of the males, and the unspoken order is carried out. We often see sentries changing shift under this undemocratic system, no questions asked.

Imagine us humans in this situation. We would all be arguing about who had done more sentry duty, and how Joe over there had only done half an hour yesterday!

The big males act as the troop's defence, and should any danger threaten, they immediately rush to the source. They are always on red alert, and scramble at the first note of a troop member's alarm bark. The females dash to grab their young, and move to the middle of the troop for protection. Leopards need to bound in quickly and snatch a baboon before the troop rallies. One male baboon is no match for a leopard, but three or four are. ■

Baboons constitute only a small portion of a leopard's diet; the leopard finds it easier to hunt less alert species, like impala. As well as having superior senses, baboons can unite to drive off an attacking leopard.

A stalking leopard crouches, keeping a low profile, and hard to see in the high grass of the vetiveria.

BABOON BEHAVIOUR

Once, on returning to camp at midday, we saw a puff of dust out of the corner of our eyes and, looking around, we saw a leopard who had just brought down an impala. Very unusual at this time of day. As the impala was feeding near baboons, the big males rushed to the scene and succeeded in driving the leopard off. They formed a semicircle around the bush into which he had retreated, and remained there, barking furiously. They certainly had too much respect to venture any further. After a short while the impala, who was only stunned, stood shakily up and walked away, apparently none the worse for its experience.

Often the baboon males seem to yawn, but most of the time, like the hippos (see page 69), they yawn to show their weapons – their teeth – and they normally do so close to a rival. It is much the same as the behaviour of our males when trying to impress a potential girlfriend. We seldom fight and, even when we do, it is normally brief, with minor wounds inflicted on both sides. Most important, we keep our egos intact. Watch a baboon, sable, impala, or any animal encounter of this kind, and you will see the same basic behaviour re-enacted.

A troop of baboons is formed of many little units, probably related, or just friends. Close friends become grooming partners, a means for special bonds to be formed. When it comes to mating, it looks as though even the youngsters have a quick go, but come the time for peak conception and it will be the big dominant males who mate with the females in oestrus. A female's oestrus is advertised by her swollen and pink rear. During this time she often stands in front of a male and presents her rear to him.

Baboons do not see well in the dark and, with the continual leopard threat, they maintain sentry watch right up until they climb up into the trees for safety. Up there they sleep in a closely knit group, so they can fend off any attackers.

Like the baboons, cheetah, kudu, and other creatures use the termite mounds as vantage points. Swainson's francolins utilize them as elevated perching spots from which to proclaim their territory with their loud, raucous calls. Many animals use the mounds as natural salt licks (the termites bring many minerals from deep down to the surface). This is important for plants, too, as the soils have been turned and aerated, and new minerals brought up to the surface for them. ∎

An amorous dominant male baboon with a female and her young.

The long hair of the baboons makes it easy for the juveniles to hold on to their mothers – the older ones can catch a lift, jockey-style, on their mothers' backs.

*Under the rising full moon baboons on
sentry duty stand guard over their troop
as they move into the trees to sleep.*

A python waits in ambush in a tree, tongue out, scenting the air. A bushbuck comes down to a pan to drink, and the python waits for it to finish and move beneath it. The python, camouflaged in the dappled light by its black-and-yellow markings, will slither silently forward and drop straight on to its prey, biting, and coiling itself around the animal to crush and kill it.

JUNE

A cheetah putting a termite mound to good use as a lookout post.

The rock monitor lizard (also called a leguaan) in a tree.

By the end of June the rut is well over, and Zimbabwe is into its coldest time of year, the temperatures occasionally plummeting to 41°F (5°C). But the temperature variation during the day is great, and it stays this low for only a short time, rising quickly after sunrise. By midday it will be back around 77°F (25°C).

This cool season is a time of beautiful, cloudless days and almost perfect daytime temperatures. It may become overcast for a day or two every so often and, if we are really unlucky, it may even drizzle. During these times some of us have the cheek to complain about the weather!

Noticeable by their absence are the insects, for although there are always some around, most of them – particularly those that annoy, like mosquitos – have gone into hibernation. Gone are the days of sleeping under nets on wet sheets because of the heat.

This is a good season for us to see animals, but it introduces a time of hardship for the herbivores. The small inland waterholes are beginning to dry up, as is the food supply for both grazers and browsers. There is now a gradual movement of animals down on to the floodplain.

The tawny eagles have started to nest. Now that the trees have dropped their leaves, except for the odd evergreen, their nests are difficult to conceal. In fact, it is quite impossible to hide such large, untidy nests built from small branches, so the eagles place them right at the top of tall trees, often knobthorns, to make their access really difficult. They can do this because the sun is mild at this time of year, so they do not need any shading for their chicks. The other eagles, who breed later, do need shelter, so they breed lower down in the canopy, when the trees are in leaf.

Shy, secretive antbears come out after nightfall to dig holes into termite mounds in search of prey. Antbears live entirely on termites. The many holes they dig make useful homes for warthogs, hyenas, and porcupines. Antbears also dig directly down into the earth in search of subterranean termites. They can probably smell them, though this is no guarantee that each excavation will prove successful.

A black sparrowhawk in flight.

The white-backed vulture builds a nest out of sticks.

The tawny chicks grow feathers on their backs quicker than other eagle chicks, which gives them some protection from the sun, and camouflages them from the prying eyes of species who might think of them as a welcome snack. The young chick lies flat in the nest to give the impression that it is unoccupied. (Like several eagles, the adults hatch two chicks, but the stronger one kills the weaker – this is called the Cain-and-Abel struggle.)

We also see the white-backed vultures nesting now in the Zambezi valley. They time their breeding so that by the time their young make their greatest demands for food – when they are almost fully grown – carcasses are most likely to be abundant. This is, of course, at the end of the hot, dry season. ∎

Fish eagles mostly survive on dead or floundering fish. They also feed on rodents, smaller birds and, occasionally, they may eat carrion.

THE HYENAS

UNRECOGNIZED HUNTERS

A hyena moving its young. They sometimes need to do this because of pressure of numbers in the den, or danger there. The new-born cubs are jet black, which makes them difficult to spot when peering into potential dens.

Little remains of a carcass after everyone has had their fill. Even the bones are crushed by the teeth and powerful jaws of the hyenas. A hyena's stomach juices can digest skin as well as bones.

For the same reason, the hyenas and wild dogs are denning now. Once the rains have come, and the glut of young is over, the cubs must be able to run with the adults. Hyenas seem most fequently to use old antbear homes as dens for their cubs, with spare holes being used by friends or relatives. The frequent usage of dens at these times means that the hyenas leave a highway of spoor leading to them. As the hyenas are mostly nocturnal, if you follow the spoor early in the morning, it will lead you to the den. ∎

Just like the wild dogs, hyenas have been much maligned over the years. It is often said that hyenas only scavenge around lion kills, and that they kill only the defenceless and the weak. How wrong this is – as the German Hans Kruuk discovered during a four-year research project. He studied the hyenas of the Serengeti Plain and the Ngorongoro crater in Tanzania. He discovered that hyenas are efficient killers, pulling down animals as large as zebra and wildebeest. In the areas he studied, the bulk of the large herbivore kills were made by hyenas, and he found that it was the lions who scavenged more frequently.

The hunting normally took place at night, so the whooping, cackling and giggling that always accompanies a hyena kill would attract the lions for an easy meal. They would rush in and steal the kill for themselves. As there are no predators to challenge them, the lions could afford to take their time over the meal, and were often still at the kill in the morning. Tourists arriving at the spot would then be greeted with the picture of the noble lions at their kill, surrounded by cowardly, scavenging hyenas.

With great stamina at their advantage, hyenas need large open plains on which to hunt by running down their prey. Lions, by contrast, need a wooded habitat, so they can stalk their prey. Mana Pools favours lions more than hyenas, who do more scavenging than hunting here. ∎

*A hyena about to feed on a leopard killed
by another leopard in a territorial fight.*

Zebras have individual sets of stripes; no two zebra are identical. These stripes may help to blend a herd, making it difficult for one zebra to be singled out in a chase.

A leopard sharpening its fearsome claws on a tree. This may also be a means of marking its territory.

A hyena basking in the sun outside its den.

HYENAS ON A RAID

Things do not always go the lions' way. One evening we were woken by a series of whoops, interspersed every now and then by shrieks, giggling, and outbreaks of deep leonine roaring. We rigged up a spotlight and jumped into a vehicle to go and investigate. A very short drive away we found two lionesses on a zebra kill, and surrounding them, eleven hungry hyenas.

The hyenas were all in their extreme aggressive posture: all had their tails right up and bent slightly forward. They mounted attack after attack, retreating each time the lionesses retaliated. Every now and then they would take a break and rest for five minutes or so. Suddenly one would jump up and the rest would follow suit, the whole chorus starting up again. They became increasingly more daring, until eventually, the pressure too great, the lionesses relinquished their kill. The hyenas chased them for a couple of yards, then quickly turned back to secure their prize.

Like wild dogs, hyenas kill by disembowelling their prey, which, if small, literally disappears in front of your eyes. One night we watched four hyenas dig out a warthog. It must have dug itself into a rather shallow overnight hole, and the hyenas were quick to take advantage. As they caught him, he squealed for a mere second or two before he was ripped to pieces and disappeared in a cloud of dust and hyenas. In minutes, each hyena had grabbed a last morsel, and was settling down to finish the remainder of its snack in peace.

Sights like that engender a great respect for the savagery out there, and make a profound contrast with the peace and calm that seems to reign in the daytime. Night is another world.

Hyenas are very territorial, and mark their territories by forming middens where, at random times, the whole pack defecates. These middens, called latrine areas, mark territory belonging to the pack, not to an individual. They are conspicuous, as the high calcium content of the faeces causes them to turn white when dry.

The jaws of the hyena are exceptionally strong – second in crushing power only to the great white shark. Their skulls differ from those of other predators in that they are not rounded, but taper to a central ridge. The muscle that enables them to crunch up large bones is attached to the bone either side of this ridge.

These animals also mark their territory by

THE BUSH BY NIGHT

secreting from their anal glands on to pieces of grass, and scraping backwards with their paws, thus leaving behind more scent from their interdigital glands between their toes. You see domestic dogs do this near another dog's house, or during a confrontation with neighbouring dogs. However, hyenas are more closely related to cats, and have their own family, the Hyaenidae.

PICKING ON THE WEAK

Another incident of savagery in the bush occurred when an old female hyena was almost ripped to pieces by the rest of the pack. The females are bigger than the males, probably so as to be able to defend their cubs against any form of male cannibalism. The faded spots on this female's coat indicated that she was old. Apparently with no warning, the others suddenly set upon her then left her for dead. Colleagues who watched this incident say her feet were almost bitten off, and large bites covered her body.

After a while the poor old girl hobbled down to the Zambezi to try to drink, and of all the bad luck, a small crocodile had a go at her. Not surprising when she was so badly wounded; animals quickly recognize a sick or weak quarry. Lions, wild dogs and hyenas always select such a victim prior to a chase.

We once saw a lioness being darted to remove a snare that had caught her around the neck. The second the drug began to take effect, and she started behaving strangely, the big male attacked her and had to be driven off. Another time we brought home our dog, who had just come round after an anaesthetic at the vet's surgery. We put it down on its feet, still slightly shaky, and the other dogs attacked it, though they had all lived together for five years. ∎

A buffalo snare made of thick wire blended with twigs and branches to make it look more natural. The local Africans would set it on one of the paths buffalo follow down to the water.

An injured lioness was subdued by darting for treatment.

Predators and prey must be able to see well at night for survival, or else take refuge up trees or in holes. A substance used in sun creams to reflect harmful ultraviolet rays is guanin, which is the same substance found in the reflective parts of the rod cells in the retina of the eye (*see* page 40). In the bush, guanin reflects back your torchlight when you shine it into animals' eyes at night. The eyes of prey and predator are easy to distinguish by reflected torchlight: the eyes of prey are wide apart for good all-round vision; predators' eyes are close together for a direct line of sight.

If you venture out at night, a whole new world opens up. A spotlight exposes the eyes of shy creatures you normally would not see, hidden as they are in the thicker bush. The multiple eyes of impala herds look like distant cities. Of the smaller creatures, the white-tailed mongoose, the only nocturnal mongoose, can be glimpsed, leaving no stone unturned in its search for prey. Civets and rusty-spotted genets are common. They are often referred to as cats; their spotted and striped coats do make you think of cats, but they belong to the mongoose family. Servals are a true spotted cat, and exceptionally beautiful, often to be seen on the edges of the vetiveria in which they live.

Caracals, or African lynxes, are occasionally seen at night, but they are rare in this area. By contrast, the scrub hares are ever-present, seeming to succeed under almost any conditions. ∎

When a spotlight is in the vicinity, impala eyes reflect the light back, looking rather like the lights of a small city, and thus betraying their presence. Leopards take advantage of such spotlight viewing, and often attack the dazzled animals, making use of their unfair advantage.

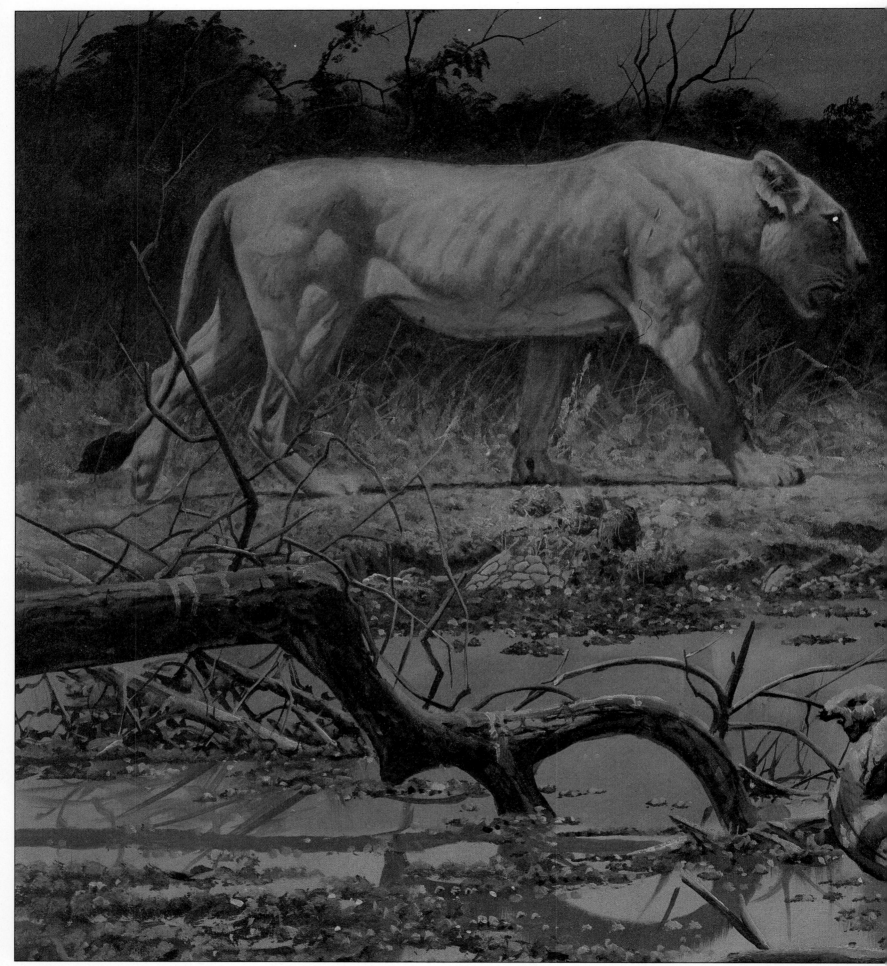

In the dead of the bush night a lioness returns from hunting to collect her cubs from where she left them beside a pan. As they pad quietly beside fallen trees debarked by elephants, their eyes reflect the light from our spotlights, but they ignore it. A couple of hours before sunrise the lioness will attempt to kill again.

THE STARS AND SOUNDS OF NIGHT

A serval kitten playing with a tortoise.

A lion may roar for either of two reasons: the first is to signal to pride members where he is located; and secondly to act as a warning to other lions to stay away.

A brilliant canopy of stars rises above the bush on most nights, and in winter the Southern Cross and Scorpio are dominant in the early evening, along with the Magellanic Clouds, which are just visible and are separate galaxies from ours. You can look for the equilateral triangle formed from Arcturus in Bootes, Spica in Virgo, and Denebola in Leo. In summer you can see Orion, the Seven Sisters, Gemini, Eridanus, and the river of stars that joins Achernar with Orion. The ancient Egyptians saw this river as the Nile, whilst the Babylonians saw it as the Euphrates.

As if all this were not enough, there is a cacophany of sound. The water dikkops' plaintive call dies away like a fading battery. (As this call fades as quickly as some of the new batteries available in the Third World, some people jokingly call it the 'Third World battery bird'.) Sit quietly for fifteen minutes and you will almost always hear a hyena whooping somewhere, or a lion roaring. Should this be nearby, the sheer power in that sound is incredible to hear.

Three small owls (the Scops, the barred and the pearlspotted) will be calling a great deal from the end of June, in the evening and early morning, joined in the early evening by the

A pels fishing owl with a catfish he has caught.

giant eagle owl with its gruff, grunting call. Should you be camped near the Zambezi river, you may also witness the eerie call of a pels fishing owl. The prettiness of this owl is rarely seen – it is strictly nocturnal and preys mostly on fish, caught fish-eagle style. Because leopards call for shorter periods than lions, you tend to hear them less often. Their call sounds just like someone sawing wood, and lasts for about five saw-strokes.

On moonlit nights there seems to be very little activity, and we must presume that the nocturnal animals feel less secure with the bright light and must tend to operate in the thick bush. They are also less vocal during these times, impalas during the rutting season being the exception. ■

Hares live in forms, which are often in the open, and not more than a depression in the ground.

A genet - a small mammal related to mongooses - keeping a low profile at night-time, when it hunts.

Cheetah reach speeds of between sixty and seventy miles (about 100 kilometres) per hour over short distances. They can make sharp twisting movements to match their prey because of their long muscular legs and flexible spine. These cheetah are hunting in ideal habitat, the mopane scrub around Long Pool, an area modified by elephants into stunted vegetation (good for ambushing), and grassy plain.

THE CHEETAH

Cheetah cubs tone up their reactions and muscles in play.

All predators, except for wild dogs and cheetahs, are nocturnal. Cheetah prey on the smaller herbivores, or subadults of the larger, and in Mana Pools they kill mainly impalas. They are the only predators whose top speed exceeds that of their prey. But in this case the prey has greater stamina, and the cheetah must close with the animal within 400 yards (350 metres), or it will be exhausted by the effort. Cheetahs kill by biting and holding on to the throat, so that the prey suffocates.

Once the kill is over, the cheetahs may take up to ten minutes to recover. They are very timid, so their kills are frequently appropriated by other predators, the lion and hyena in particular. For this reason, cheetahs hunt during the day – so as not to attract the attention of any predator sleeping nearby. When calling her cubs to the kill, the cheetah has a bird-like call.

Cheetahs are not strong animals and never stand their ground when threatened at a kill. All they have to rely on is their speed, so they cannot risk injury. The other predators, if injured, can rely on members of their pack or pride to do the hunting, or on their ability to stalk closer, with a resulting shorter chase. Cheetah are rapidly declining, and the reduction of their habitat is one of the prime reasons. The other is tourism: because they are extremely timid, and never return to a kill once driven off, insensitive safari operators are further adding to their decline by driving as close as possible to kills.

Cheetahs are territorial and are frequently seen using termite mounds and prominent trees as places for marking territory, as well as for lookout posts. They are often to be seen hunting as a family before the fully grown offspring

move off. As an aid to their survival, the coats of the young animals make them resemble ratels (honey badgers) at a distance. Cheetahs require open plains with good grass cover to hunt on. Apart from the mopane scrub around Long Pool (*see* pages 142-3) the present Mana Pools habitat does not favour them, hence the poor population. The plains are heavily grazed, affording them little cover for their approach. Much of the wooded area has scrub underneath, which breaks up their stride and thus reduces their speed, which also makes this habitat unsuitable for the cheetah. ∎

Cheetah have to be very careful when hunting. They must avoid injury, as they survive on their lightning-like speed alone. They would rather surrender kills than risk injury defending them.

Two cheetahs sit beneath a wild mango tree on the edge of the plains, perfectly camouflaged among the creepers of a flame combretum and the plains grasses. They are watching a lion who has taken over their prey. Cheetah kill more than they eat, because prey is often stolen from them by other predators. They never fight, because they cannot risk injury, so when challenged for a kill, they retreat.

LANDSCAPE BY ELEPHANTS

As well as dislodging the Faidherbia albida *pods, elephants also like to eat the bark of the tree, which contains many desirable minerals.*

The largest pan of Mana Pools is called Long Pool (*see* page 6). Just south of the pool area is a long plain, and on the western end, large mopane woodland, which suddenly becomes mopane scrub, clearly stunted by elephants feeding. Most of the trees are reduced to near elephant-mouth height. The demarcation line must have something to do with a soil change making the trees on one side more palatable. As you move eastward, they start to thin out more and more. Due to feeding pressure some of the scrub must have died. Still further on it gradually becomes grassland, with just the occasional mopane stump remaining. This is a good example of how elephants modify a habitat, and in this case are benefiting grazers. This habitat also suits the cheetah, which thrive on open grasslands.

Remembering the saying that the only constant in life is change – maybe the elephant pressure on the albidas is a part of a general changing and drying out of the floodplain, due to the river ceasing to flood here. The river has deposited a great deal of sand some twenty-five miles (forty kilometres) downstream on the Zambian side, making a big floodplain-type area. Numerous albida seeds have been deposited here, partly by the river, and partly by the wealth of seeds in the elephant droppings. The elephants digest the fleshy part of the pod, but the seeds pass through them undigested. Over the past five years an albida forest is forming and the trees are now about ten feet (three or four metres) tall, and it seems as though a new floodplain is being formed.

Even when the elephants are breaking down trees, they are planting many more via their droppings. They play a particularly important role in the dispersal of various seeds and when the seeds germinate they will already have some compost around them to help them into growth. At places on the floodplain, the clumps of albidas can be seen, which are the remains of old islands, where the river once was. As the islands formed, the wind blew grass seeds on to them. Because no animals could reach them, the next dry season they had a good grass cover.

Elephants then swam across to feed on the grass, and by dropping dung they planted the albidas. By the time the river had eroded northwards enough for the island to become mainland, the albidas were big enough to be a benefit to the community, with their winter shade and protein-rich pods.

A big bull elephant feeds on about 450 lb (200 kg) per day, but only about forty per cent of this is digested, the rest being passed out. This process speeds up the nutrient cycles. Through the termites and dung beetles the nutrients are returned to the soil for use as a kind of natural fertilizer to be taken up by the plants again. ∎

JULY

The albidas look really splendid now, their fresh green canopies forming in many places an almost closed canopy over the now dry, yellow grass. They are all in pod, and the pods are now starting to fall off the trees on to the ground, where they form a much-needed protein boost for many animals during this time of diminishing food supply.

The elephants love the pods and shake the trees to dislodge them. Occasionally, after shaking the tree, no pods fall, and they seem almost embarrassed before moving on to the next tree, scarcely believing their bad luck. They also eat the smaller albida branches, by plucking them off the tree. Later, when the browse line is just out of reach, they have to balance on their hind legs like circus elephants to reach them.

When the young elephants find the branches too high to reach, they follow the big males closely and, ever so politely, steal a piece whenever they can. They are funny to watch, for they sidle slowly closer to the bigger bulls, as though the last thing in the world they want is a taste of that branch. The bigger bulls are fully aware of this ploy, although they pretend not to be. Suddenly they will swing at them and the young bulls retreat quickly.

The albidas provide plentiful shade, an important requirement at this time of year because the majority of other trees are leafless. The albida bark contains minerals that are in great demand by elephants, who at this time of year debark many trees by their feeding habits. Baobab trees, with their pure fibre inside, are much in demand. ■

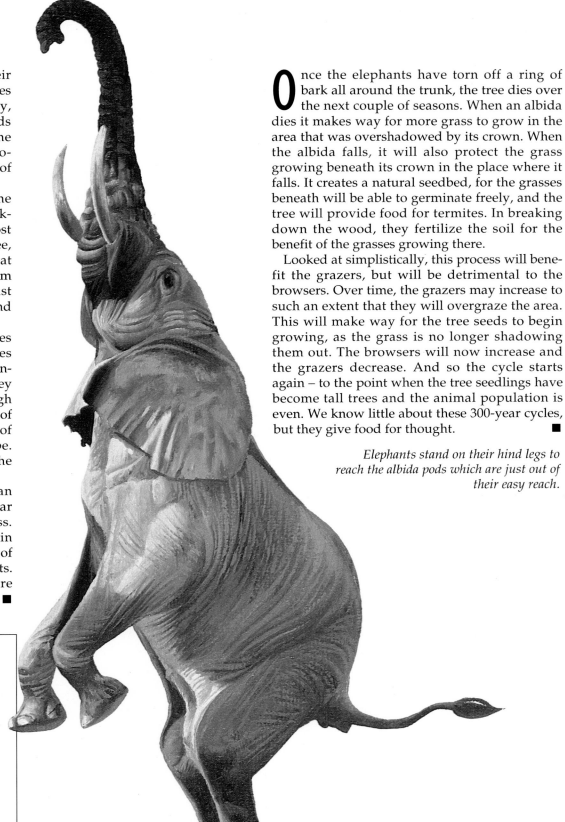

Albida pods are shaken from trees by the elephants, or fall naturally to the ground. These pods provide much protein at a time when food is becoming scarcer on the floodplain.

THE BENEFITS OF FALLEN TREES

Once the elephants have torn off a ring of bark all around the trunk, the tree dies over the next couple of seasons. When an albida dies it makes way for more grass to grow in the area that was overshadowed by its crown. When the albida falls, it will also protect the grass growing beneath its crown in the place where it falls. It creates a natural seedbed, for the grasses beneath will be able to germinate freely, and the tree will provide food for termites. In breaking down the wood, they fertilize the soil for the benefit of the grasses growing there.

Looked at simplistically, this process will benefit the grazers, but will be detrimental to the browsers. Over time, the grazers may increase to such an extent that they will overgraze the area. This will make way for the tree seeds to begin growing, as the grass is no longer shadowing them out. The browsers will now increase and the grazers decrease. And so the cycle starts again – to the point when the tree seedlings have become tall trees and the animal population is even. We know little about these 300-year cycles, but they give food for thought. ■

Elephants stand on their hind legs to reach the albida pods which are just out of their easy reach.

August in the dry season. A whole colony of carmines can be seen nesting in the holes on the bank of the Zambezi. A lone bull elephant looks out across the river from within a group of debarked wild mangoes. The trees in the background are called raintrees, because insects suck the sap and then rain it down as droplets.

ZEBRA FAMILIES

Female zebra have a gestation period of about twelve months, and give birth to a single foal. These births usually occur during the rainy season, when there is plenty of cover and food around.

Zebras are found in small family units numbering seven on average. As the stallions mature, they are forced out and, like the impalas, these young stallions form bachelor herds, seldom numbering more than four in a group. They may be identified by a lack of foals within the group.

The family units are built up through stealing yearling mares from other groups. Oddly enough, when the mares come into oestrus for the first time, they develop a special walk, which excites the stallions to fight for them. This is nature's way of stopping inbreeding.

The family units are stable, and when a mare is brought into one, she remains there for life. This why she develops the special oestrus walk only on her first oestrus (and does not use it subsequently). If you approach a family unit, you will see the stallion immediately, as he will always put himself between any potential danger and the herd. It is not necessary for them to be territorial with this system, and they will often join with other zebras to form huge herds. But if you look closely, you will see individual families within.

Lions are the zebras' main predator. It is not uncommon to see zebras who have escaped from an encounter with a lion wearing huge gashes on their haunches as testimony. When these wounds heal, they often do so with the black and white stripes unaligned. When you see a zebra with its ear or tail bitten off, the chances are that it is a stallion wound, for they often fight among themselves. ∎

FAMILIES ON THE FLOODPLAIN

The elephant cow herds are now spending more time on the floodplain, and not returning the great distance back into the jesse. They do not form large herds here, but prefer to remain in groups of five to fifteen, with twenty being a large group.

The baboons are a great benefit to all on the floodplain, for their feeding habits are messy and they frequently knock down valuable browse and fruit for the animals on the ground. The other animals seek the baboons out for this, as well as for their early warning system, for no group of animals is more alert (*see* page 120).

The buffalo herds have swollen in size by July, as more and more herds have arrived. They consist mostly of cows and young bulls, but during the breeding season you will see a few adult bulls running with the herds. The bulls roam alone or in small groups, and spend much time wallowing in the mud. This has earned them the name of 'dagga boys', `dagga' meaning `mud'. The older gentlemen can be fairly aggressive at times, and should be treated with respect.

Recently, however, it has been the buffalo cows that have been giving people more trouble. Last season (1991) we captured some 400 buffalo and, for the first time, moved them across Lake Kariba on a huge ferry. One buffalo cow continually charged the open modified Land Rovers, getting her horns into every conceivable place. They were all pretty much exhausted by the end of their journey, and on releasing them, this cow was the last one out. She wearily struggled to the top of the bank, and paused to look back. Then, to our total disbelief, she charged the ferry.

The calves can be equally aggressive. On another occasion, weak calves, who could not keep up with the herds, had been left behind to die. We would drive up to them, and after catching them, treat them with a chemical to remove the millions of ticks on them. After a shot of vitamins we would send them on their way. Even these little calves, barely able to run, would charge the vehicles.

The elands have also begun to appear in larger numbers, and they will retrim the browse line on all the Natal mahogany trees. It is almost a characteristic feature of Mana Pools that the evergreen mahoganies look as though the bases of their crowns have been cut with a knife. This is a sure sign that eland frequent the area.

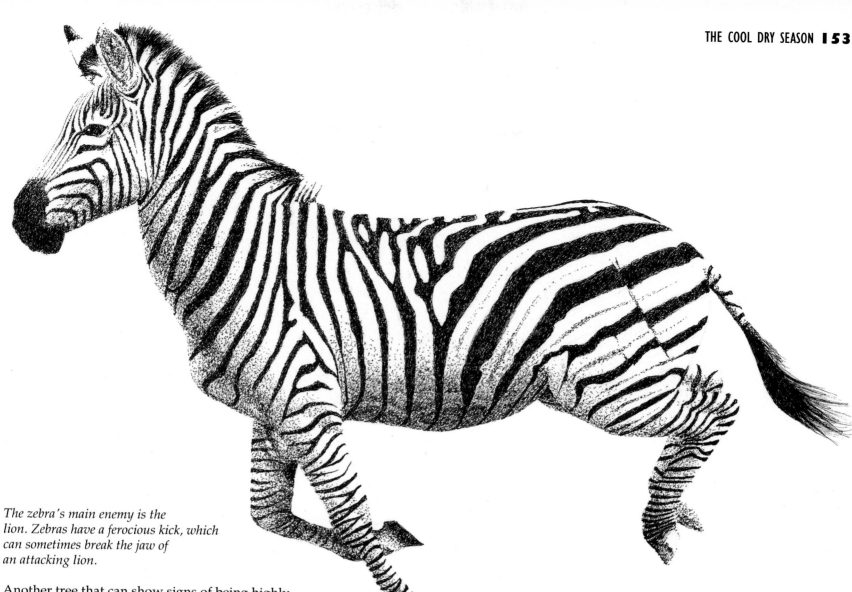

The zebra's main enemy is the lion. Zebras have a ferocious kick, which can sometimes break the jaw of an attacking lion.

Another tree that can show signs of being highly browsed is the *Faidherbia albida*. One cannot over-emphasize the usefulness of this tree. It is a quick grower and provides plenty of shade. It also has a paradoxical, seasonally inverted foliage cycle, by being leafless in the rainy season, which means it is different from other African savannah trees. It is a pioneer colonizer of newly laid-down alluvial soils, and therefore young albida trees have to be fast-growing in order to avoid complete submergence in subsequent floods.

The tree is useful to man in that the tap root does not compete with field crops for nutrients or moisture, so crops can be grown right up to the trunk. As the leaves are shed at the beginning of the rains, crops planted around its base are not deprived of sunlight. These leaves rapidly decompose and provide a remarkably rich fertilizer.

The albida soils are high in nitrogen, because of the leaf-fall and the flowers (between them accounting for fifty per cent of the nitrogen provided), the pod-fall (accounting for thirty-eight per cent) and the tree itself when it dies and provides dead wood and bark (accounting for fourteen per cent). ∎

Zebra wounds often heal in such a way that the stripes are put out of alignement.

A bachelor herd of zebras enjoys the shade in an inland pan on the edge of the mopane woodland. At midday in the hot dry season, temperatures are searing. Shadow stripes between the broad stripes on the rumps of these animals identify them as Burchell's zebra. In the foreground, a skull is all that remains of an impala kill. A red-billed hornbill has its nesting hole in the mopane tree.

Buffalo bulls play-fighting, their huge handlebar horns can be used to deadly effect in serious battle.

Eland are the largest of the antelopes, and both males and females have horns.

ALBIDA TREES AND WARTHOGS

As the water table recedes, these pioneer trees eventually rot and die, giving way to the longer-established vegetation, such as the mahoganies, ebonies and leadwoods.

As the grazing diminishes, warthogs get down on their knees to reach the very bases of the grasses, as well as the tubers and bulbs below. They start mating now so as to begin their four-and-a-half month gestation, and time the birth of their young with the November rains. The male follows behind the female, with that wicked look in his eyes. While making a noise that can only be described as sounding like an old single-cylinder Lister engine, he trots

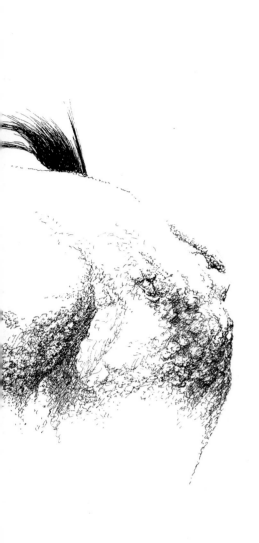

behind the female and tries to rest his head on her rump. Away she goes again, and so on, until eventually she stops and allows him to mount.

The theory is that the continual touching gets the female used to the male's touch, until eventually she is conditioned enough to let him mount. Sable and steenbuck court in a similar fashion, the male walking behind the female, tapping her politely between her back legs. She may walk a couple of paces, then stop, and the same happens – she eventually becomes used to his touch. Is it not just the same with us humans? We always find reasons to touch, pat and hug a prospective partner during courtship. It's a theory, anyway. ∎

Buffalos rub their horns in the mud and against the bushes. Eventually, through continued use, the horns become worn down – a sign of old age.

A buffalo with her day-old calf. Buffalos calve all year round but births peak during the wet season. The calves are born within the herd and are able to run with the herd after a short period of time.

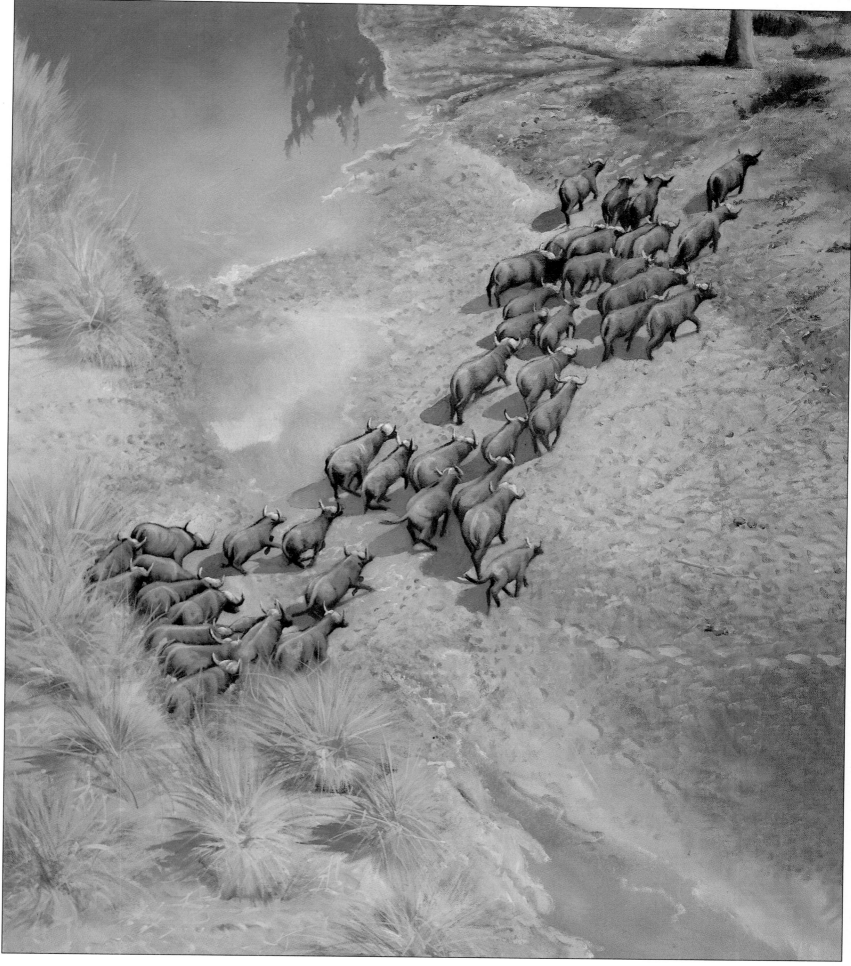

A buffalo cowherd is startled into
stampeding out of the vetiveria grass of
the floodplain in August. The herd may
be anything from 20 to 500 strong.

A buffalo herd resting in the evening on the edge of the mopane. In the foreground is a depression that will become a pan when the rains start.

*A male leopard waiting for the
precise moment to launch his attack.*

Sausage trees generally flower in August, their flowers providing food for animals like impala and kudu. Whilst still on the tree the flowers are visited by bats. Here a buffalo is sniffing one, its nose supplying moisture for the ever-present flies.

AUGUST

Some humans rely on the honeyguide bird to lead them to honey. The local villagers then light a fire under the bee hive, which drives the bees away, so that they can retrieve the honey in safety. The honeyguides look on nearby, hoping to get a small commission.

The ratel (honey badger) has forefeet and claws for digging purposes – it also uses these as formidable weapons of defence. This is a fearless animal, which thinks nothing of fighting back against large predators like the lion.

With the arrival of August, everything starts to prepare for spring, which is anything from two weeks to a month away. The dawn chorus of bird calls is now in full throat. Just at sunrise you hear the ground hornbills booming in the distance. The three small owls (the Scops, pearlspotted and barred) are calling furiously, along with the giant eagle owl grunting high up in the tall trees. Lizard buzzards, African hoopoes, honeyguides, and striped kingfishers, all add to the sound. All the woodpeckers – the bearded, bennets, cardinal, and golden-tailed – are also calling territorially everywhere you go. Another method they use to proclaim territories is to tap on hollow branches, which amplify the noise. To avoid confusion, each species has a different tapping frequency.

Shortly after sunrise the carmines come out of their nests in holes in the riverbanks, and perch nearby, enjoying the early morning sun. They turn the bank almost to crimson where they perch, and their continual calling can be heard a long way off. The weavers are building furiously, and the colonies are full of demonstrating males, hanging from their nests and fluttering their wings to try to attract a mate. There are two main types of weaver: the lesser-masked, and the spotted-backed. You can tell them apart, if you cannot see their backs, by the colour of the eyes. The lesser-masked has a yellow eye and the spotted-backed a red one.

Once the males have paired with a female, they continue to build, and the colonies may expand to become really large. Once the females have laid, there is always the danger of cuckoos parasitizing them. The Diederiks cuckoos have arrived from the tropics by this time. The female sneaks into the unattended nests, removes one of the host's eggs, and lays one of her own. Diederiks' eggs are normally fairly close in colour to those of their hosts.

The Klaas's cuckoo is here too, parasitizing the sunbirds. Both cuckoos are calling territorially, the Diederiks is particularly prevalent, and extremely aggressive if you try to mimic its call. If one should fly over you and you give its call, it will promptly turn 180° and land in a tree nearby to search for the other male who has the cheek to invade his territory. The emerald cuckoo, the third of the three small green cuckoos, arrives with the rains to coincide with the breeding season of its host, the bleating warbler. It is the most beautiful of the three, being green and gold, and although it calls from the treetops and in the dense foliage of that time of year, it is seldom seen.

The immaculate nests of most weavers are in total contrast to those of the white-browed sparrow weavers, who usually build their untidy, spiky nests on the western side of a tree. The theory behind this behaviour is that they live in their nests all year round, and they need protection from the easterly prevailing wind.

HONEYGUIDES – FACT OR FICTION?

Honeyguides are very active, calling frequently, and are well known for their habit of guiding humans to honey. They will land in a tree next to you and sit chattering, trying to lead you away. The idea is that once you reach the hive, after raiding it you leave a portion behind for the bird as a reward. We have followed them on occasions, but have lost interest after about an hour. On one occasion it was the bird who lost interest, and suddenly flew back over our heads and disappeared – so much for the theory!

These birds are reputed to lead honey badgers, of which there are many in Mana Pools, to bee hives. The badgers rip open the hive, their skin being impervious to stings, and remove the honeycombs. The comb and some grubs are left for the bird. We often wonder at this relationship as we have never seen a honey badger climb a tree. Honeyguides are diurnal, and the honey badger is largely nocturnal. They are the only animal whose spoor shows five toes. They generally trot around minding their own business, but let something aggravate them and they are scared of nothing. They have even been known to attack the wheels of a vehicle that was following them. ∎

You can recognize spotted-backed weavers by their red eyes (the lesser-masked weavers have yellow eyes). A male weaver will normally build the nest, then the female lines it.

THE FLOWERING SEASON

THE SEED CO-OPERATIVE

Ground hornbills resemble large black turkeys. These birds make a deep booming sound, which is normally heard at the first sign of dawn – rather like a sergeant-major waking up the troops.

(right) *The carmine bee eaters nest in colonies on the high banks of rivers; their diet consists of grasshoppers and other small insects.*

Sausage trees, with their lovely straight trunks, are ideal for carving out dugouts, the wooden canoes of the African fishermen. It takes much balance to remain afloat in one of them, let alone to fish from it.

The sausage trees have started dropping their big maroon flowers, which become meals for the kudus and impalas when food is rapidly disappearing. We even watched a buffalo sniffing hopefully at one of the flowers, but he thought better of it and marched on his way. Leopards greatly favour these trees, their canopies providing perfect concealment. They are ideal to ambush from now, when animals are gathering beneath for the flowers. During this flowering season, we once had four different sightings of leopards in sausage trees in one week. On one occasion a French guest of ours exposed the leopard's hiding place. As he walked across to inspect the flowers, out jumped a leopard. The guest's surprise was capped with a single word: 'Merde', which translated means 'Gee Whizz', or 'Wow' – or so we were told.

The bush is alive with flowers of all types and colours. The knobthorns are abloom with cream-coloured, spiky blossoms, the pink jacarandas with their canopies covered in pink, wild mangoes in orange, cassias in yellow, raintrees in mauve, and the flowers of the flame combretums have turned the tops of many albidas into fire. The shaving-brush combretums with their spiky blooms add white, while the loranthus parasites add splashes of red. Add the brilliant sunbirds attracted to all these, and you have something close to heaven. ■

Like any business of this type, the seed dispersal industry has various agencies handling the dispersal of the different fruits. Civets control the bird plum and ebony agencies. If you look at a civet midden, you will see all the seeds within. Baboons do monkey fingers, sausage trees, and albidas. Elephants share the albida agency, and are the prime distributors. They also act as agents for many others – garcinias, torchwoods, marulas, and ilala palms.

Once you understand all this, the bush has new meaning. We can now see that a civet planted this, or a baboon planted that, and an elephant planted all these. In fact, the four different clumps of torchwood seedlings tell us that approximately four months ago an elephant passed here. They are the places where each of his droppings landed, and by being this far apart, the elephant was walking slowly as he did them. If one finds clumps of marula seedlings, we will know that this elephant came from an area a long way off, as no marulas grow on the floodplain. ■

At sunrise baboons climb down from the trees and, in winter, sit warming their backs in the sun.

Leopards rest in trees, where they are totally out of danger, and have a good vantage point from which to survey the plain unobserved. The chosen trees are normally fully leaved to provide welcome shade, and it is quite unusual to see a leopard lying exposed to the sun in the midday heat.

THE USEFULNESS OF TREES

The baobabs are very important at this time for the elephants, as they supply not only food and water, but shade inland as well. From 10am onwards every day, one might see a small herd of elephants huddled together under the shade of the trunk of a large baobab. The baobab is a very good friend to humans, too. The fibrous tissue holds water, which you get by chewing. This fibre makes the best rope of any of our indigenous trees. The pods contain fruits, and cream of tartar – rich in vitamin C – and the seeds may be roasted and crushed for coffee. The pods are ideal water containers, and the leaves are edible, tasting rather like spinach. The bark may be used to make soles for sandals, and the often large holes in the trunk may contain water stores from previous rains.

The sausage trees are pollinated by fruit bats, just like the baobabs. Sausage-tree fruits are used commercially in the cure of skin cancer. Another tree found in this area is the feverberry croton, which was once used for the treatment of malaria.

Yet another useful plant in the recent past has been the strophanthus. This is a scrambling shrub that has a really strange-looking pod, and an equally strange-looking flower. The seeds within are ideal for wind dispersal, and contain Strophanthin, a drug that acts upon the heart, and was once used as an arrow poison. Cures for many ailments come from trees and one can only imagine how many more are still waiting to be discovered. ∎

The local tribes in the Zambezi valley commonly make dugout canoes from sausage trees.

Carbon dating has put some baobabs' life spans as up to 3,000 years. These trees flower from October to June/July.

The fruit of the sausage tree yields a substance that is effective in treating skin cancer.

*The helmeted guinea-fowl are usually
found in large flocks, except when breeding.
They feed on seeds, fruits and insects, and
spend most of the time on the ground,
although they can fly when necessary.*

PLANT DEFENCE

A fruit bat hanging upside-down in a crevice of a baobab tree.

A civet under threat, responding in a defensive mode. These nocturnal creatures normally live in holes in the undergrowth, or in disused antbear holes. Their diet consists of birds, reptiles, small mammals and insects. The civet used to be persecuted heavily because the secretions from its scent glands were used in the perfume trade (synthetic materials are now used instead).

Plants have many modifications that help deter the browsers, thorns being the obvious and best known. On some plants, thorns are modifications of the stems, and on others it may be the stipules, which give paired thorns. You will often see thorns much in evidence up to the height of the highest browser, and above this they tend to grow less and less. The ilala palms and the flame acacias have wicked hooked thorns; if you are really pressed you can modify these thorns into fish hooks.

The aquatic mimosa, which grows on the banks of the Zambezi river in places, extends its fine leaves fully open for maximum photosynthesis. Let some browser feed on it and the browser's touch will cause the leaves to shrink and expose the thorns beneath. The leaves now look completely unattractive and wilted, and make a movement rather like louvres suddenly being opened.

There is also the well-known trick of certain acacia trees, which produce excess tannin, thus rendering themselves unpalatable, so that they are not over-browsed. In an experiment it was found that even the unbrowsed trees in a neighbouring plot increased their tannin output without being touched. How was this message passed by the trees?

LIFE IN THE TREES

The mopane trees in particular provide welcome holes for the many squirrels in the Zambezi valley. Many other animals use them; the dwarf and banded mongooses have been seen using the dead ones. These social mongooses are insectivorous, and forage in groups. Normally the mongooses live a solitary existence and prey on snakes as part of their diet.

The ground hornbill also uses holes in mopane trees for nesting. The male diligently feeds his mate in the nest, but she can sometimes leave, with the mate taking her place. The red-billed hornbills use these trees early in the summer to breed in. They differ from the ground hornbills in that the female is sealed into the nest with clay, and a narrow slit remains, through which the male feeds her. She moults all her feathers to line the nest. She needs the security of a sealed nest to be safe from predators, as she is now flightless.

As the eggs hatch, the male has to work hard to supply enough insects for everyone. The flights of alates (*see* page 51) make his job easier. When the chicks are nearly fully grown, the female has regrown all her feathers, and breaks out of the nest to make space for the young. She reseals the nest and helps the male with the feeding. Eventually, when the young are mature, they break out and leave. ∎

MOCK CHARGES

Whenever animals feel threatened or even just uncomfortable about something going on in their environment, they may attempt to oust the intruder by a mock charge. This is almost exactly the same reaction we would have if we suddenly found a herd of cows had got into our garden and was destroying the plants. We would probably rush out, shouting and waving our arms, and pick up sticks or rocks to throw at them. Once they had moved out of our territory, the fuss would all be over and we would sit down and continue with what we were doing.

This is precisely what wild animals do frequently. The more stressed they are, the less tolerant they become and the more likely they are to behave like that. It is their only way of saying 'please leave me alone'.

You instantly recognize this behaviour when an animal suddenly looks up at you with a 'this is the last straw' look in its eyes, draws itself up to its full height, and runs towards you. If it is an elephant, it trumpets as it runs; a lion growls; a rhino snorts; a buffalo bellows; a hippo runs towards you, mouth open, spraying water in front of him as he goes – his equivalent of kicking up dust.

Very rarely do animals act like this, and there must be a fair amount of provocation to initiate such behaviour. It can be very disconcerting, however, when you arrive on the scene, in all innocence, just after someone else has just provoked an animal to its limits and left. However, if an animal is not to be tangled with, the second it is aware of your presence it will spin on you, running at top speed, an expression of apparent intent to kill you on its face. You will certainly not mistake this look. ∎

To make themselves look bigger and more menacing, elephants shake themselves and thrust their heads up, with their ears flapping.

In the dry season elephants feed largely on baobabs, often causing the trees to collapse after a couple of seasons. The elephants chisel into the tissue to reach the moisture and minerals in the fibres. These two bulls have their heads up and ears out – a sure sign that they have been disturbed.

CLOSE ENCOUNTER

I f one wants to approach elephants, the best method is to wait until they are near a large fallen tree, of which there are many at Mana. By getting behind, the tree you make it difficult for the elephant to reach you. Elephant cannot jump over anything that is more than about two foot (sixty centimetres) high, so an obstacle like a tree will stop any charge. If caught in the open with nothing to get behind then the best course of action is to stand your ground and shout. To turn tail and run would be suicidal.

This theory is fine with bulls, but we are far more apprehensive with cow herds, as they are much more aggressive.

Many charges are from playful young bulls. These bulls sometimes take to charging moving vehicles, running at the same speed. We find that if a driver slows down then so does the elephant. The young bulls probably would not know what to do with a 4 x 4 even if they did catch up with it.

Most people find this 'near brush with death' terribly exciting. We believe that crossing the road in busy traffic is far more dangerous – like trying to move between herds of elephant running in top speed in both directions. But in the bush it has a special quality, and so these experiences are embellished, beer in hand, around the camp fire at night.

Canoe trips on the Zambezi river are becoming a regular sight, and they set the stage for more survival stories. It is now the hippopotamus' turn to scare innocent nature lovers to death. These animals doze and sunbathe in the shallows of the river where they can stand or lie. The deep water, their safety, is always close should there be any hint of danger. Canoeists come gaily breezing past on the deep side of them and, of course, the hippos all make a beeline for the deep. Watch the saucerlike eyes of the canoeists and their frantic pulling to `get away' from the animals, and you can imagine their stories of having `survived the attack'. ■

An elephant testing the wind – should he smell you and feel threatened enough, he may decide to charge. Most times this turns out to be a mock charge but occasionally it can be with deadly intent.

An elephant dusting in the evening light –
like covering oneself with talcum powder.

Some irritated animals make mock charges to tell you to leave them alone. This bull elephant must have been extremely provoked, since he charged straight out of a breeding herd. You would generally expect a cow, normally the matriarch, to do this. When she does charge it is very foolish to stand your ground, as you can with most charging bulls.

PREPARING FOR THE SPRING

Inland from the river, the elephants have been digging in the dry river beds to reach the water table which can sometimes be as much as six feet (two metres) down. These diggings enable other animals to survive in these areas without having to make the long trek to the river to drink. The elephants also compact the floors of the many clay waterholes, stopping water leakage and keeping them deep. These little waterholes benefit the whole community during this dry time.

Flocks of queleas, known as the avian locusts of Africa, are now to be seen in large numbers feeding across the plains. The flocks make a rolling motion in flight, which is caused when the birds feeding at the rear fly to the front of the feeding flock, as they exhaust the seed supply at the back. Some years, after successful breeding seasons, they can literally block out the sunset as they make their way to their roosts. We timed one flock flying unbroken across the sky for twenty-eight minutes, and that was just a one-off count. How these birds avoid mid-air collisions is truly amazing.

The birds of prey do well now, as there is little cover for their prey. African hawk eagles, a predator of guinea fowl, surprise their prey as they swiftly fly low through the trees. Crowned eagles, who have recently become residents on the floodplain, have been recorded preying on vervet monkeys. The immature birds are much lighter than the adults, but are just as capable of lifting prey this size. The monkeys are forced by the lack of food away from the tall trees, the riverine areas in particular, to forage. This makes them far more vulnerable to predation.

Francolin are also targeted by various raptors. The riverine is home to the natal francolin, which seldom ventures away from this habitat; the other species of francolin also adhere strictly to their type of habitat: the crested francolin are found in the thickets away from the rivers; and the swainsons live in the open bush savannah.

During a two-week period camped by the river, we heard the natal francolin start calling just before dawn each day. So accurate were their initial calls that you could have set your watch by them. ∎

A mopane squirrel building a nest in a mopane tree.

Buffalo have a keen sense of smell and normally run from danger. When one approaches a herd, the bigger bulls stand facing you, watching every move. They will even walk a few paces towards you, sniffing the air, and trying to confirm what they see.

The nuts of the mopane tree provide food for the mopane squirrel.

In the dry season elephants find water by digging deep into the river-beds.

THE HOT DRY SEASON

The hot dry season falls between September and November. It is Zimbabwe's spring – and the hottest time of year. Intense heat is followed by massive cloud build-up, leading to impressive electrical storms. Temperatures centre on the 105°F (40°C) mark. The heat is not humid – you will probably feel hotter during the hot wet season, when temperatures are lower, but humidity far greater. The heat is building up. Heat waves start to shimmer across the floodplain.

There is very little inland water now, save for the occasional spring, way back on the escarpment. Only the deepest, most retentive waterholes still hold water.

SEED DISPERSAL

The winds have been blowing strongly since August. They are nature's way of distributing the summer's crop of seeds, many of them specifically designed for wind dispersal. The strophanthus seeds hang on the wind like parachutes, and are often dispersed great distances away. Dust devils – whirlwinds – swirl their way across barren plains like minute cyclones, carrying the seeds still further.

The animals are also busy dispersing seeds. While the fleshy, palatable outer cover is being digested, the animal that ate it is travelling on – the protected seed passing through its digestive system, to be excreted out of the body by the time the animal has moved some distance from the original feeding place. ■

Bushbuck are difficult to see, as they blend in so perfectly with the thick bush.

An immature crowned eagle chases a
vervet monkey. These primates normally
live on big trees in the riverine area, but in
the dry season they are forced to forage on
the ground away from the trees.

(overleaf) *The secretary bird is the only
terrestrial raptor in existence. It marches*
across the grasslands searching for
rodents and reptiles, and kills snakes by
fierce stamping. These birds have tough
scales on the legs to protect them from
snake bites.

Open-billed storks nesting in tall trees not far from the river are outlined against a blood-red African sunset.

These butterflies are pieridae whites, seen here getting moisture from a pile of elephant dung.

A pair of male pride lions rest from marking their territory on the edge of the Zambezi River. On a rare overcast August day they catch the last rays of the late-afternoon sun, their manes swept dramatically back by the strong winds prevalent at this time of year.

A tortoise in the aftermath of a hot burn in the late dry season. The fire swept over it as it huddled in its shell, and it walked off unscathed after the fire had passed. Some nearby droppings look untouched, but others were burned to a cinder, and will crumble and blow away on the wind.

BUSH FIRES

A haze hangs heavy over the whole region. It is caused by the many bush fires burning, not only across Zimbabwe but also over in neighbouring Zambia and Mozambique. Fires have been part of the natural system since time immemorial, and their effects are very beneficial. Scientists have worked out that fires occur naturally about once every four years. They are normally started by lightning – the hot dry season is the time of year when nature produces electrical storms – but they also occur as a result of the spontaneous combustion of damp, decaying matter producing heat.

DELIBERATE BURNINGS

In the management of game parks, fire is used as a tool to change the habitat to that desired by the managers. If you were experiencing a decrease in your grazing population due to the encroachment of many woody plants, you would give the area a hot-burn to kill the shrubs and promote more grassland. A hot fire needs lots of ready fuel and a good wind. August, September and October are the driest months of year, and the windiest. This is when a wildlife manager will introduce a hot-burn. Nature does it herself with lightning at this time.

If a wildlife manager found that his browsing population was decreasing due to a lack of shrubs, a cool-burn would be the answer. This is a fire started when some green grass remains at the beginning of the dry season, and it burns with little or no wind. It is a gentle, slow-moving fire, which burns coolly around all the shrubs and trees, not harming them, but suppressing the grass, giving the new woody seedlings a chance to get ahead before the grass shadows them out. Nature uses spontaneous combustion for her cool-burn management program. Cool-burns occur naturally when there is still some moisture around in April or May.

Fires eliminate all the rank tissue that remains at the end of the dry season. This will always be unpalatable, and when it remains over into the next season it shadows out any new growth coming through, and will thus lessen the carrying capacity of that immediate area. Some seeds germinate better for having been burned first, and some are actually totally dependent on fire for germination.

Many diseases are destroyed by fire, and it also controls the tick population. When animals overgraze an area, many unpalatable plant species invade, so there is less to eat, and the condition of the herbivores deteriorates. This makes them far more susceptible to disease. Tick populations now explode, helping to spread the diseases through the populations. The weakest animals will die. A hot fire in the region rids it of parasites and diseases, and will set back the development of unpalatable plant colonies, and encourage the more desirable ones to return. This will be more likely if the number of herbivores feeding on them is reduced.

In 1990 the whole Zambezi valley burned for the first time in many years. There were just too few people to control the fires, which had been started by farmers burning out rodents, or burning for grazing for their cattle.

These fires, along with the winds blowing dust into the atmosphere, create the blood red sunsets, for which Africa is famous. Let us hope these blood-red sunsets are not depicting Africa's swansong. ∎

A late-evening bush fire occurs shortly after the wet season has ended. This is a cool burn, as there is little combustible material, and much of the vegetation is still drying. The dry season hot-burns travel for miles, their flames reaching as high as forty feet (twelve metres), and may last for months. In the bush, lack of fire can be just as damaging as too much fire.

THE LIONS

*A lioness resting in the trees –
unusually – to get away from biting
insects. She may also feel a
welcoming breeze up here.*

*A buffalo resting during truce-time
at midday.*

The lions are commonly seen at this time of year, and they seem to be everywhere. There are normally many matings around August, so that the cubs are born in the rainy season, when there is plenty of cover. During oestrus, the dominant male will remain in close attendance on the female, mating frequently over a 24-hour period.

Young males are tolerated in the pride, and will be forced out at around three years of age if conditions are bad. This may also happen to the lionesses, although it is less likely. These young lions then become nomadic, and are forced out to the marginal areas by the other prides. When territories become vacant through the death or disappearance of the pride's males, or when a weak male can be successfully challenged, these young males can lay claim to a territory.

The greater the lion population, the more they roar. The roaring tells other lions whether a territory is occupied or not, and it is a very efficient spacing system.

Each pride has, on average, two pride males

A lioness initiates mating by rubbing up against a male.

and four lionesses. The pride males may often be seen walking together, away from the pride as they go about their territory, marking it. This entails scent-marking the bushes every now and then with their urine. Other lions will not be allowed within the territory. The females chase out females, and the males oust other males. A nomadic or estranged lioness will gradually be tolerated within a pride, whereas a lion would have to fight for acceptance. These foreign lionesses suffer many oustings but the severity of the attacks gradually lessens with time. Frequent submissive gestures also help in their eventual acceptance within the pride.

The primary role of the male pride lions is that of maintaining the pride's territory, and thus making it a safe place for the females to breed in without being harrassed by nomadic lions. Although they do kill for themselves on occasions, the lions feed more often on the kills made by the lionesses.

In the daily hunting cycle, midday is the time for a truce and a siesta. Even the prey species drop their guard and doze or chew the cud. Only in exceptional circumstances is this rule not observed. ■

A pair of young lion cubs at play.

Lionesses on heat have been recorded mating once every fifteen minutes over a 24-hour period. At these times the mating lions are oblivious to all else and, if disturbed, the males may act aggressively, but will quickly break off any charge to return to the important task at hand. Mating normally takes place at the end of the dry season, so that the cubs are born during the wet season.

The black-maned lions have killed a young zebra, which might have been sick, or separated from its parent herd. Males do kill for themselves, but also rely on appropriating the kills of the females.

Their main job is to protect their territory against other males who might threaten their young. These big males are in their prime, aged between five and eight years. In the foreground of the picture is a weaver's nest that has fallen into the pan. The nestlings would have been quickly eaten by catfish.

MOURNING ELEPHANTS

CROP RAIDING

Elephants have been known to try to revive dead friends.

Elephants display bizarre behaviour over the death of other animals, particularly their own species. We often read of them covering carcasses of dead elephants. A friend of ours has a slide of a dead elephant completely covered with branches put there by other elephants. Cynthia Moss, in her book, *Elephant Memories*, mentions several incidents with elephants' skeletons, which in some cases may be carried some distance from the original site. Tusks in particular incite much emotion, and there are many records of elephants carrying them away from carcasses and even breaking them.

Once we had to put down an elephant that had suffered a broken pelvis. After the unpleasant task was completed, we skinned it (as is the normal procedure) and put the skins at the back of our house. Shortly afterwards, other elephants began to push down our fence and enter our yard. This happened on three different occasions. On the first two we found the skins scattered about. They had been fondled and smelt by all the intruders. The third time they walked away with them, and some of the hide was found as much as half a mile (800 metres) away.

Elephants also rally together to help other elephants in difficulty and distress, lifting them with their trunks or feet, and propping them up, an animal on either side, to keep them on their feet. We recall an elephant bull that was shot for crop-raiding in one of the tribal areas. When a road to the carcass was made, it was discovered that the bull had been pushed at least fifty feet (fifteen metres) by the remainder of the herd, who had returned to try to revive him. ∎

Elephants appreciate the benefits of a national park and know what may befall them outside its boundaries; the continued shooting of elephant crop raiders over time has taught them. They learn quickly that the shootings take place only in daylight. In one area we were at we would notice several elephants feeding within a couple of miles of the park boundary. Come last light, across the boundary they would go, raid any maize crops in the vicinity, and be back inside the park's boundary – where they knew they would not be shot – by first light.

For the tribespeople, their limited crops are their food, their only means of survival in these remote regions, and elephant raids force them to defend their crops with their lives. For example, two old men heard elephants in their maize, and after beating drums to try to scare them off, they resorted to running within range and throwing rocks at them. One bull suddenly swung at them, and after easily catching the nearest one, threw him on the ground and tusked him so many times that the body was cut in half. The bull then carried half of the body about 200 yards from the field. The bulls then returned to the same maize field for four consecutive nights, and the bull responsible returned to the spot where he had dragged the body, and sniffed the area before continuing his crop-raiding.

Finally he was shot, and it was then found that his body was covered in suppurating sores, perhaps the result of a fight. This was probably why he was so aggressive. It is generally the cows who show such aggression, being extremely protective of their young. ∎

RECEDING WATERS

Perhaps as a sign of grief, or respect, elephants sometimes cover their dead with branches.

An elephant acknowledges death.

As the water in the last-remaining pans recedes to the pan's centre, animals have to plough through the mud to reach it. They often get stuck, and die a long, lingering death. One day we came across this grisly scene while walking on the floodplain. A young bull elephant was stuck in a pan, and he looked completely exhausted from his efforts to free himself. We decided to try to help him, and spent the next two days to that end. One of our group remained with him overnight in an effort to keep at bay the hyenas who were trying to eat him alive. Eventually, using two Land Rovers and a tractor, we pulled him out – very painfully, for him, because of the clay's suction. Unfortunately, he died just after we finally got him out. It was sad to lose the battle after so much effort.

In areas where there is no perennial water, many animals die around the waterholes. It is thought that these concentrations of carcasses gave rise to the myth of elephant graveyards. ∎

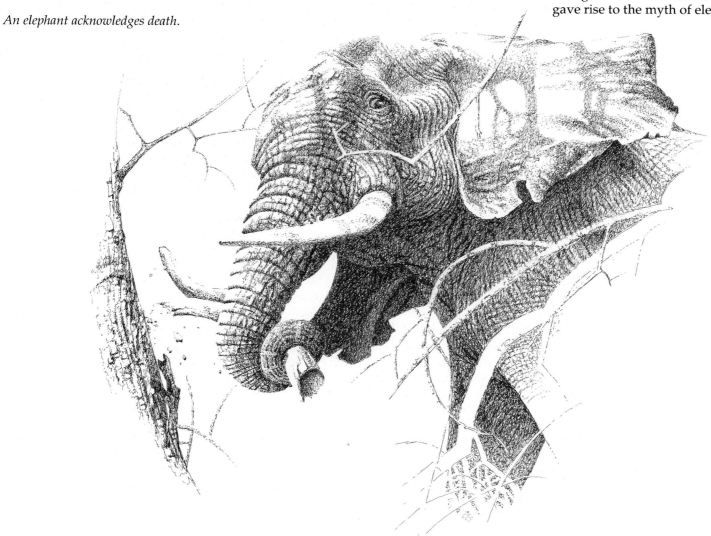

There are no such things as elephant graveyards. Elephants have been known to spend time with the remains of friends or relatives. It is not known if the deceased are recognized through this touching and smelling. But how can one explain the scattering of bones by the living elephants – almost like humans scattering the ashes of our loved ones?

OCTOBER

An elephant cow and her calf in bad times. Note the sunken forehead on the cow. The calf, too, is in poor condition, and has lost part of its tail to a predator. Predators are quick to take advantage of any weakness.

The zebras fare the best of all the grazers, and always seem to be in good condition, This is due, as previously mentioned, to their ability to utilize the coarse fibrous tissue of grass that the other grazers cannot eat. When the bulk of the zebra manes have drooped, due to the exhaustion of their fat reserves, then you can be sure that the rest of the grazers have long since perished.

In the marginal years many carcasses litter the bush by October. Nature is harsh in maintaining the survival of the fittest. One group of animals that seems to profit from poor conditions is that of the scavengers. People look on this group with disgust, forgetting how important they are in the system. With the many carcasses lying around during this, the harshest time of year, the scavengers' role is vital. They keep clean an area that would otherwise be a breeding ground for disease. As the larger carnivores move off, having had their fill, the smaller carnivores rush in to pick through the remainder of the carcass. They are followed by the vultures, who feed on what is left. If the animal was of average size then the hyenas eat many of the bones, leaving only the back bone, some of the ribs, and the skull. Much of the hide is eaten by the dermestes beetle, and the outer cover of the horns is broken down by the larvae of the horn moth, which burrow into it. They pupate in cocoons they spin on to the outside of the horn.

The bones of a larger animal, such as a buffalo or an elephant, may take a couple of years for the weather to break them down.

Blistering heatwaves fill the October days, the temperature often reaching the forties. The earth is barren. Everything is waiting for the rain. At night we sleep on sheets dampened with water to make the hot nights a bit more bearable.

Shortly after the sun sets, when only a pale glow remains in the sky, flocks of double-banded sandgrouse wing their way to the water with rapid flight. They drink at dawn and dusk. These inhabitants of the dry regions breed at the height of the dry season, and the males have specialized breast feathers that absorb water for the chicks to drink on their return to the nests.

Stinkbugs are also attracted to the last raintree blossoms, and their buzzing may be heard in the background. Such moments are wonderful. When a lion suddenly roars, or a hyena whoops nearby, there is nowhere else on earth one could want to be. ∎

WAITING FOR THE RAINS

The clouds begin to build up into huge cumulo-nimbus. Electrical storms become more frequent and increasingly more impressive. Each day seems to be the one when the rains are finally going to break. The whole atmosphere is electric. When it rains, everything goes berserk. Animals jump and spring about everywhere. We run round in the rain, behaving like children. That night, everyone sleeps their best sleep of the whole year. The fallen rain brings a wonderful smell, and a feeling that is indescribable.

A couple more good, hard rains and the whole cycle begins again: the game migrating off the exhausted floodplain; the resident population left behind; the recovery of the immediate area and the springing into leaf of the grasses and trees; the lungfishes breaking out of their dry-season homes beneath the baked earth. Everything renews itself. ■

CHANGING ECOLOGY

The local people living in the Zambezi valley – never a very large population in the past – originally concentrated themselves along the Zambezi River. Today, these numbers are increasing, leaving less land as natural bush. These small-scale naturalists and fishermen have been taught no land management or agriculture skills, and one can foresee the erosion due to riverbank cultivation as being a major problem in the future.

The damming of the Zambezi River at Kariba forced many of the river fishermen to move their homes either upstream or downstreeam from the Lake. As well as affecting the local populace in this way, the formation of this new lake also had some major effects on the river's ecology downstream, particularly on the Mana Pools floodplain.

To complicate things further, another wall was built downstream from Mana Pools at Cabora Basa in Mozambique. This has turned the Zambezi River into a far more sluggish body of water, with no real flooding taking place. The river is unable to carry its silt load as it used to, and so deposits much of it in the middle of the river, forming islands there. This has resulted in the water running much more quickly along the banks of the river – which increases the erosion there. With the banks continually caving in (whole *Faidherbia albida* trees collapse into the river as their foundations erode) we now have a very much slower river, occasionally exceeding a mile (two kilometres) in width. ■

The breaking-down process of horns is expedited by the invasion of horn moths.

Zebras are only in poor condition when their manes have collapsed (as here), indicating that the energy reserves of fat beneath them have been used up.

The elephants in a herd know their range intimately. The older animals, having experienced at least one serious drought in their lifetimes, know exactly where to find the last secret waterholes and food, or the best hiding places when persecuted. All information gathered from experience is passed down to the younger animals through the generations.

TERMITE PRESSURE

Since the river has ceased to flood its banks, there has been a massive increase in termites, who were previously drowned by flooding waters. So big is their population now that they are competing very strongly for grazing with the floodplain herbivores. The result is a great increase in woody plants and unpalatable herbs, thus reducing the carrying capacity of the grazing.

Fires, so important in these systems, do not occur anymore, as there is nothing to burn towards the end of the dry season. This lack of cumbustible material is in part the consequence of the termite pressure on the area. The termites eat the dry and dead grass in the dry season – as do the herbivores. There is little living grass to be found other than that found along the river's edge, and on the islands. The soils of the floodplain are just the right composition for the termites, which could not really colonize before, because of the flooding.

The hot fires of the late dry months used to encourage grass growth as they set back or killed woody plants and unpalatable herbs. Now that there are no fires, the result is that the grazers eat the grass right down, allowing sunlight penetration so that the seeds of woody plants can flourish. As the woody plants take off they overshadow the new grass trying to take root. This overshadowing means that sunlight does not filter down to the grass. This occurred around 1988 when Mana Pools was covered in unpalatable weeds. Tourists on their first visit to Africa could not help but notice the lack of grass cover. This spells disaster for the grazers. The carrying capacity of the land, that is, the amount of food that land can carry for a group of animals or even a specific species, had been reduced. This means that the woody plants dominate the area and, as they do not bind the soil as well as grass, there is more run-off when it rains. With this lack of water penetration, the soils become drier, so the good palatable species of grass start to die out, and are replaced by unpalatable herbs and grasses which favour these conditions. The grazers do not eat these so there is little food available to them.

The widening of the river has, however, benefited many other creatures. Fish that prefer the calmer, shallower water have increased, and the habitat of many wading birds has been extended. More grazing has become available for the island-hopping creatures such as buffalo, elephant and waterbuck. ∎

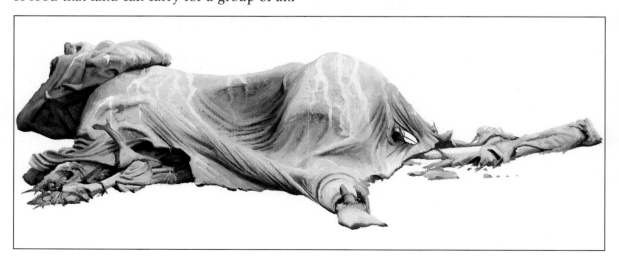

The carcass of a poached elephant.

*An African hunting dog runs across a pan
early one morning, its tail-tip a clear sign.
When the rains break, the lungfish will
dig themselves out of the mud where they
have hibernated for the dry season.*

Hyenas lie among the mopane stumps on the plains late in the afternoon in the hot, dry season. This is cheetah country. Around them are the old elephant tracks from the previous wet season. The skull of a poached rhinoceros lies in the foreground. The mopane trees in the background have just flushed, stimulated by the temperature increase. The animals look expectant, ready for change. Streaks of lightning flash across the sky, contributing to the build-up of tension, a sure sign that relief is on the way.

UNCERTAIN FUTURE

The future of the wildlife – both plant and animal – in Zimbabwe – remains uncertain. Lack of funding, lack of organization, over-population (both human and animal) all combine to make the situation a volatile one.

In addition, the already fragile ecology is visited by droughts, floods and disease. It is difficult for local people to make animal conservation their priority when their very day-to-day existence is a struggle for their own survival.

The animals of the National Parks can yet be saved, but much needs to be done, and the responsibility lies with the wealthier western nations as much as with the Zimbabwe government. A combined effort, with the west providing funding and scientific expertise; and the Africans offering local knowledge, commitment, and a willingness to incorporate conservation into their way of life could help to tip the scales in the animals' favour.

TSETSE FLY– SCOURGE OR BLESSING

Local fishermen split caught fish open, smoke them, and then take them by the sackfull to local towns to be sold in the markets.

Tsetse flies are still very common over much of the Zambezi valley. These must be the hardiest flies on earth. When they bite you feel a sudden searing pain. The bites usually occur around the lower legs, with feet and toes taking much of the punishment.

Unlike other flies, tsetse flies breed very slowly: only one egg is produced every seven to ten days. The larva hatches inside its parent, and is born only when ready to pupate. The larvae are very susceptible to parasitism and predation at this stage.

The presence of these flies, though annoying, is fortunate for the wilderness areas for the time being. They keep out the cattle, which represent rural development and the end of the wilderness, of which there is precious little left. The prognosis is poor, however, as an expanding population will eventually claim these areas, with or without cattle.

ANIMAL SLAUGHTER

The arrival of the Great White Hunter began the start of the slaughter of wild animals in Africa. But the slaughter continues with the large quantities of illegal weapons which have filtered into Africa, falling into the hands of ever-increasing numbers of poachers. Tsetse-fly eradication programmes have also been responsible for over 650,000 game animals shot in this part of Africa between 1919 and 1960. This slaughter was done to aid the expansion of the farming sector, to ensure that in the corridors (strips of land along the valley's edge, ten miles [sixteen kilometres] wide, enclosed by a fence to contain the fly) there is no risk of Trypanosomiasis, a disease carried by the tsetse fly and fatal to livestock. Tsetse flies also carry a human form of this sickness, known as sleeping sickness. This debilitating disease has, however, been largely eradicated. Maintaining these corridors and further expansion of the tsetse eradication programs, led to the use of DDT (*see* page 93) within the areas contained by the corridors and excluding the National Parks. The effects of the chemical are still not fully known. What is known is frightening enough, because predators at the top of the food chain are worst affected. Much has already been published about the decline of the African fish eagle and the black sparrowhawk.

THE FLY TRAP

The Zimbabwe Tsetse Department has designed an ingenious trap to help eradicate the fly and diminish the need for DDT. The trap consists of black cloth, as tsetse are attracted to shade, or dark colours. The trap moves on a central pivot as the cloth catches the wind, and this movement further attracts the fly. The fly is also drawn to the trap by the smell of acetone, contained in a bottle on the trap. The smell of this acetone resembles that of a cow's breath. This is the main lure for the fly, which then lands on a screen between the areas of black cloth. This screen is impregnated with an insecticide (Deltamethrine). The fly has just to land on the screen for the poison affect it, and will die later.

SPONSORSHIP AND RESPONSIBILITY

As we write, the EEC is still sponsoring the tsetse programmes in Zimbabwe, but no one wants to take responsibility for what happens to these areas after they have been cleared. These areas are taken over by the rapidly expanding rural population, which is increasing at just below four per cent per year – one of the largest population increase rates in the world. While people must have land, its proper use thereafter is crucial. We do not have any to spare. The people moving on to this land have, by and large, received little or no practical training in land usage or conservation. Their wealth is in their cattle and goats, which are kept in numbers far exceeding the carrying capacity of the land. So with the continual overgrazing, desertification is the result, and the people simply move on to a new area of land, with the same end result. ■

THE BENEFITS OF WILDLIFE

Severe overgrazing problems are not caused by wildlife. When an area is overgrazed in the wilderness the game simply move off the area and go elsewhere, allowing the grazing to recover. If the grazing shortage is widespread then the population dies back in proportion to what grazing is available. This too allows the area to recover. In addition, game animals are self-sustaining, because of their natural immunity to disease, whereas cattle cost their owners money to maintain.

THE FIGHT AGAINST POACHING

As tribal people struggle to make ends meet, they have turned to indiscriminate hunting and snaring in the bush. This has, unfortunately, led to a very lucrative trade in illegal rhino horn and elephant tusks.

A few years ago it was recognized that Zimbabwe was the last major stronghold of black rhinos in Africa. Today there are pathetically few left – most have fallen victim to the guns of the poachers. The Zimbabwe National Parks are able to field only a very small number of anti-poaching units, due to an extreme shortage of government funding. Yet there are many dedicated people who would be more than willing to offer their services in the anti-poaching campaign, but as they are not government employees they are not allowed to do so.

Zimbabwe's non-governmental private sector has embarked on a sustained utilization of

wildlife in the tribal areas in an effort to try and save the remaining wildlife. They hope that by giving the wild animals a monetary value to the locals, then the locals will in turn protect the game. This has been done by offering a substantial sum of money to the chief and his people for hunting rights. Hunting clients are then brought in to hunt on a commercial basis, and for each animal shot the relative sum of money is paid to that rural council. Amongst the animals hunted are dangerous game – elephant, buffalo, lion and leopard. These animals were previously hunted or snared by the locals, as they com-

At the turn of the century (1900) there were estimated to be about 5,000 elephants in Zimbabwe – today there are more than 50,000. The Great White Hunter would have found it more far difficult to locate elephant in the old days than would be the case today.

Some poachers with a hippo they have killed. The meat from these animals is said to make very good eating.

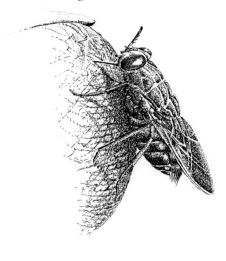

A tsetse fly, carrier of sleeping sickness, biting a toe.

Tsetse-fly traps have been placed a couple of hundred yards apart, extending in a line for miles, to help eradicate the tsetse fly. If it proves successful, then the Zambezi valley and its wildlife would be vulnerable to further settlement by a rapidly increasing population.

peted directly with the tribesmen's livestock and crops. Now any such loss incurred by these people will be offset by the amount of revenue generated by commercial hunters. Any poaching done now is by outsiders, and these poachers are robbing directly from the local community. Thus an ironically beneficial situation has developed. The locals, who used to be poachers themselves, now police their neighbourhood on the lookout for snares and unwanted guests. Who better than the local community to do this – they know every nook and cranny in the area, and all the tricks of the trade.

OVERPOPULATION OF ANIMALS

In some areas it has been necessary to trim the numbers of some animals, especially the elephant, because of the pressure on the habitat. This can be done by capturing and relocating animals, or by destroying them. The killing of animals in this way is called culling, and is carried out by the employees of the National Parks. The calibre and credibility of the National Parks' staff is second to none. They are not hired killers, but dedicated conservationists, who hate doing this (often very dangerous) job. One person we know of, who has since left the Parks,

has had to shoot over 10,000 elephants to date. He remains anonymous, as it is not a figure to brag about – but a job that had to be done. Imagine how terrible it must be to have to shoot elephant calves, who remind us so much of our own little ones.

The culling generates a great deal of money, which *should* be ploughed back into conservation. Everything, from the hides to the meat, is sold, but the money makes its way into the government's treasury; it is, at least, placing a value on a resource. The other huge benefit is the supplying of good cheap meat for consumption by the local people. During these culling operations it is very seldom, maybe on one per cent of occasions, that any animals escape from a cull. The whole herd is shot, so there are no stressed animals left surviving, or half a family shot. A cull of a herd of fifteen elephants will seldom last longer than thirty seconds, since the members of the Parks' teams are excellent shots. There is no time for terror, for in the confusion the elephants just do not know what has hit them.

Some of the calves, if at the right age, may be saved for game farms or zoos overseas. They are drugged immediately after the rest of the herd has been culled. Although the next couple of

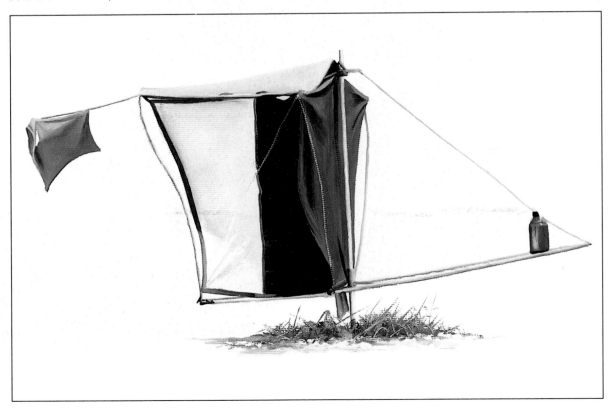

A yellow-billed kite robbing a basket. These birds also rob barbecues.

days are traumatic for the calves, they quickly settle down.

We are lovers of elephants as only people who have observed and worked closely with them over the years can be. We wonder if some well-intentioned animal rights groups have ever watched an elephant – an intelligent creature – die of starvation or thirst, or seen the horrible wounds or deaths they sometimes suffer at the hands of poachers. Ultimately, because of the pressure of mankind on the remaining wilderness, culling and capture are the only alternatives. It is impractical to drug and move whole herds of these magnificent creatures, and even if we could, to where would we move them? The wilderness is fast declining, and nobody with the power to do anything cares.

This black sparrowhawk has just killed a guinea fowl.

THE WISDOM OF THE IVORY BAN

This leopard cub has spotted a snake on the branch above .

The banning of the sale of elephant products worldwide has, we believe, sealed the fate of the elephants. No recent African government apart from South Africa has been able to control poaching within its National Parks. In the past there was a legal trade in ivory, but now that this has been banned, the ivory of the African elephant has increased in value. This means that the poachers now find the price is right, so they will risk heavy prison sentences and death to do even more hunting than before. An ivory ban can work only if poaching is controlled. The demand for ivory and rhino horn is still with us, and no ban will stop supply meeting demand. The much-publicized rhino 'poaching war' is now, for all practical purposes, a lost cause. If the almost total elimination of rhinos in Zimbabwe has been this easy, will it be any different for the elephant who now follow? Within months of the ivory ban being implemented, over eighty elephant bulls were found poached in the Zambezi Valley. We believe that this was a knee-jerk reaction to the massive increase in the black-market price of ivory. Now even the cows and small bulls are being shot. The price of ivory makes it worthwhile.

With the huge over-population of elephants in Botswana and Zimbabwe, a legitimate cull would flood the market with ivory. This would then bring the price of ivory down, and hopefully make poaching not worth the risk.

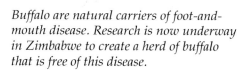

Buffalo are natural carriers of foot-and-mouth disease. Research is now underway in Zimbabwe to create a herd of buffalo that is free of this disease.

A domestic chicken on a buffalo – is this type of unnatural juxtaposition what the future could hold for us?

Anyone reading this might be rather confused – here we are saying that many elephants need to be shot annually, and yet we have the handkerchiefs out moaning about the poachers who seem to be doing the job for us.

We must explain that although elephant populations are threatened throughout most of Africa, Zimbabwe and Botswana still have over-populations of elephants in their National Parks. We have shoved our remaining herds of elephants into convenient little tracts of land where we expect them to stay. These herds have unnaturally tight boundaries within which to feed (if they go out they get shot as crop raiders) and consequently the correct ratio of elephants to acres of wilderness has changed. Elephants are prolific breeders and if left alone soon swell in numbers. Their numbers are increasing but their feeding boundaries are staying the same size. So instead of one tree out of every ten being debarked, it soon becomes one in five, and so on. Ecologist know what numbers of elephants should be in a given area. If there are too many then the environment suffers and a knock-on effect occurs, involving every species from the browsers to the grazers. The unnatural knocking down of vast numbers of trees by the elephants means the birds have fewer places in which to nest; the browsers lose out because they food they only could reach is now available to other animals, and so it goes on.

The most worrying factor is that the poachers are indiscriminate, shooting anything they think they can make money out of. The poachers have won the battle with the black rhino, and who is to say that the elephant will be any safer?

HOPE FOR THE FUTURE

All is not absolutely lost though. Many sponsors have backed a rhino dehorning campaign which is now in progress. Although two dehorned rhino have already been shot, hopefully in error, the hope is that this project might be able to save the last nucleus of our rhino population. As well as this, there are a number of game capture units presently catching excess or endangered animal populations, and re-locating them in other areas throughout Zimbabwe. ∎

After an elephant cull the calves are sometimes transferred to zoos - but the normal practice is to kill the whole herd.

*A leopard lies up in a tree, relaxed, but
ever watchful.*

FLORA AND FAUNA SEEN AROUND MANA POOLS

The common name is followed by the Latin name in italics

African Hunting Dog
Lycaon pictus
Antbear
Orycteropus afer

Baboon
Papio ursinus
Baobab
Adansonia digitata
Baphia
Baphia massaiensis
Bateleur
Terathopius ecaudatus
Bee Eater
Blue-cheeked
Merops persicus
Carmine
Merops nubicoides
Little
Merops pursillus
Swallow-tailed
Merops hirundineus
White-fronted
Merops bullockoides

Buffalo
Syncerus caffer
Bushbuck
Tragelaphus scriptus
Butterfly
Brown commodore
Precis natalica
Brown-veined white
Anaphaeis aurota
Common grass
yellow
Eurema hecabe senegalensis
Diadem
Hypolimnas misippus
African monarch
Danaus chrysippus
Scarlet tip
Colotis danae annae
Swordtail
Graphium policenes
Buzzard,
Steppe/Common
Buteo buteo

Caracal/African lynx
Lynx caracal
Cassia
Cassia abbreviata

Catfish
Clarias garlepinus
Chameleon
Chamaeleo dilepis
Cheetah
Acinonyx jubatus
Civet, African
Civettictis civetta
Cricket
Gryllus bimaculatus
Crocodile, African
Crocodylus niloticus
Cuckoo
Diederiks
Chrysococcyx caprius
Emerald
Chrysococcyx cupreus
Klaas's
Chrysococcyx klaas

Dassie
Procavia capensis
Dikkop
Burhinus vermiculatus
Dove, Laughing
Streptopelia senegalensis
Duiker, Common
Sylvicapra grimmia

Eagle
African Hawk
Hieraaetus fasciatus
Brown snake
Circaetus cinereus
Crowned
Stephanoaetus coronatus
Long-crested
Lophaetus occipitalis
Steppe
Aquila nipalensis
Tawny
Aquila rapax
Wahlberg's
Aquila wahlbergi
Egret
Black
Egretta ardesiaca
Cattle
Bubulcus ibis
Great white
Egretta alba
Little
Egretta garzetta
Elephant, African
Loxodonta africana
Eland, Common
Taurotragus oryx

Faidherbia albida
Faidherbia albida
Flame acacia
Acacia ataxacantha
Flame combretum
Combretum paniculatum
Fever berry croton
Croton megalobotrys
Fruit bat
Epomophorus crypturus

Garcinia
Garcinia livingstonei
Genet, Large spotted
Genetta tigrina
Giraffe
Giraffa camelopardalis
Goose
Egyptian
Alopochen aegyptiacus
Spur-wing
Plectropterus gambensis
Grysbuck, Sharpe's
Raphicerus sharpei

Guinea fowl
  Helmeted
  Numida meleagris
  Crested
  Guttera pucherani

Hare, Scrub
  Lepus saxitilis
Heron
  Green-backed
  Butorides striatus
  Goliath
  Ardea goliath
  Grey
  Ardea cinerea
  Rufous-bellied
  Butorides rufiventris
  Squacco
  Ardeola ralloides
Hersilia
  Hersilia bicornutus
Hippopotamus
  *Hippopotamus
    amphibius*
Honey badger/Ratel
  Mellivora capensis
Honey guide
  Indicator indicator
Hoopoe,
  African/Eurasian
  Upupa epops
Hornbill
  Red-billed
  *Tockus
    erythrorhynchus*
  Ground
  Bucorvus leadbeateri
Hyena,
  Spotted/Laughing
  Crocuta crocuta

Impala
  Aepyceros melampus

Jacaranda, Pink
  *Stereospermum
    kunthianum*
Jackal, Side-striped
  Canis adustus
Jackalberry
  *Diospyros
    mespilliformis*

Kingfisher
  Brown-hooded
  Halcyon albiventris
  Giant
  Ceryle maxima
  Grey hooded
  Halcyon leucocephala
  Malachite

Alcedo cristata
  Pied
  Ceryle rudis
  Pygmy
  Ispidina picta
  Striped
  Halcyon chelicuti
  Woodland
  Halcyon senegalensis
Kudu, Greater
  Tragelaphus strepsiceros

Leguaan
  Water
  Varanus niloticus
  Rock
  *Varanus
    exanthematicus*
Leopard
  Panthera pardus
Lion
  Panthera leo
Loranthus
  Loranthus sp.
Lungfish
  Protopterus sp.

Mahogany, Natal
  Trichilia emetica
Martin, House
  Delichon urbica
Marula
  Sclerocarya caffra
Mimosa, Aquatic
  Mimosa pigra
Mongoose
  Banded
  Mungos mungo
  Dwarf
  Helogale parvula
  Large grey
  Herpestes ichneumon
  Slender
  Herpestes sanguineus
  White-tailed
  Ichneumia albicauda
Monkey finger
  Friesodielsa obovata
Mopane
  *Colophospermum
    mopane*
Mopane moth
  Gonimbrasia belina

Nicator,
  Yellow-spotted
  Nicator gularis
Nightingale, Thrush
  Luscinia luscinia
Nyala
  Tragelaphus angasi

Nyalaberry
  Zanthoceras zambesiaca

Oriole
  African Golden
  Oriolus auratus
  Black-headed
  Oriolus larvatus
  European golden
  Oriolus oriolus
Oryx/Gemsbok
  Oryx gazella
Osprey
  Pandion haliaetus
Owl
  Barred
  Glaucidium capense
  Giant eagle
  Bubo lacteus
  Pearlspotted
  Glaucidium perlatum
  Pels fishing
  Scotopelia peli
  Scops
  Otus senegalensis

Pangolin/Scaly anteater
  Manis temmincki
Porcupine
  Hystrix africaeaustralis

Quelea, Red-billed
  Quelea quelea

Raintree
  Lonchocarpus capassa
Rhinoceros
  Black
  Diceros bicornis
  White
  Ceratotherium simum
Robber fly
  Asilidae sp.
Robin, Bearded
  *Erythropygia
    quadrivirgata*

Sable antelope
  Hippotragus niger
Sandgrouse, Double-
  banded
  Pterocles bicinctus
Sandpiper
  Common
  Tringa hypoleucos
  Wood
  Tringa glareola
Secretary bird
  Sagittarius serpentarius
Shaving brush
  combretum

*Combretum
    mocambicensis*
Snake
  Boomslang
  Dispholidus typus
  Black mamba
  Dendroaspis polylepsis
  Python
  Python sebae
  Puff adder
  Bitis arietans
Sparrowhawk, Black
  Accipiter melanoleucus
Spoonbill, African
  Platalea alba
Spider
  Baboon
  Harpactira sp.
  Bark
  Caerostris sp.
  Jumping
  Salicidae sp.
  Rainspider
  Palystes sp.
  Trapdoor
  Galeosoma sp.
Stick insect, Giant
  Phasmatodea sp.
Stork
  Abdims
  Ciconia abdimii
  Marabou
  *Leptoptilos
    crumeniferus*
  Open-billed
  *Anastomus
    lamelligerus*
  Saddle-billed
  *Ephippiorhynchus
    senegalensis*
  White
  Ciconia ciconia
  Wooly-necked
  Ciconia episcopus
  Yellow-billed
  Mycteria ibis
Strophanthus
  Strophanthus kombe
Sunbird
  Collared
  Anthreptes collaris
  Purple-banded
  Nectarinia bifasciata
  Scarlet-chested
  Nectarinia senegalensis
  White-bellied
Swallow, European
  Hirundo rustica
Swift, Eurasian
  Apus apus

Tamarind
  Tamarindus indica
Termites
  Macrotermes sp. and
  Microcerotermes sp.
Trogon/Narina
  Apaloderma narina
Torchwood
  Balanites maughamii

Vervet
  *Cercopithecus
    pygerythrus*
Vulture
  Hooded
  Necrosyrtes monachus
  Lappet-faced
  Torgos tracheliotus
  White-backed
  Gyps africanus
  White-headed
  Trigonoceps occipitalis

Warbler
  Bleating
  Camaroptera brachyura
  Icterine
  Hippolias icterina
  Willow
  Phylloscopus trochilus
Warthog
  *Phacocherus
    aethiopicus*
Waterbuck
  Kobu ellipsiprymnus
Weaver
  Lesser-masked
  Ploceus intermedius
  Spotted-backed
  Ploceus cucullatus
  White-browed
  sparrow
  Plocepasser mahali
Wild dog
  Lycaon pictus
Wildebeest, Blue
  Connachaetes taurinus
Wild mango
  Cordyla africana
Woodpecker
  Bearded
  Thripias namaquus
  Bennett's
  Campethera bennettii
  Cardinal
  Dendropicos fuscescens
  Golden-tailed
  Campethera abingoni

Zebra, Burchell's
  Equus burchelli

BIBLIOGRAPHY

Hanks, J., 1979. *The Elephant Problem*, Country Life Books, England.

Kruuk, H., 1966. 'A New View of the Hyena', *New Scientist*, 33:849–851.

Moss, C., 1975. *Animal Behaviour in East Africa* and *Portrait in the Wild*, University of Chicago Press.

Moss, C., 1988. *Elephant Memories*, Elm Tree Books, London.

Mundy, P.J., 1982. 'The Comparative Biology of Southern African Vultures',Vulture Study Group, Johannesburg.

Payne, K. B., Langbauer, W. R. J. R., & Thomas, E. M., 1986. *Infrasonic Calls of the Asian Elephant.*

Poole, J. H., & Moss, C., 1981. 'Musth in the African Elephant', *Nature*, 292:830–831.

1940, *Roberts Birds of Southern Africa*, (1st edition). Revised by McLachlan G. R. & Liversidge, R. 1985, Cape Town.

Smuts, G. L., 1982, *Lion*, Macmillan, South Africa.

INDEX